CHILDREN OF POVERTY

Studies on the Effects of Single Parenthood, the Feminization of Poverty, and Homelessness

edited by

STUART BRUCHEY
Allan Nevins Professor Emeritus
Columbia University

A GARLAND SERIES

THE EFFECTS OF HOMELESSNESS ON THE ACADEMIC ACHIEVEMENT OF CHILDREN

HENRIETTA S. EVANS ATTLES

GARLAND PUBLISHING, Inc.
NEW YORK & LONDON / 1997

Library of Congress Cataloging-in-Publication Data

Attles, Henrietta S. Evans, 1935–
    The effects of homelessness on the academic achievement of
children / Henrietta S. Evans Attles.
        p.   cm. — (Children of poverty)
    Revision of the author's thesis (doctoral)—University of
Massachusetts, 1993.
    Includes bibliographical references and index.
    ISBN 0-8153-3014-6 (alk. paper)
    1. Homeless children—Education (Elementary)—United
States. 2. Academic achievement—United States.
3. Homelessness—United States. I. Title. II. Series.
LC5144.2.A88 1997
371.826'942—dc21
                                                        97-40760

Printed on acid-free, 250-year-life paper
Manufactured in the United States of America

Dedication

To

The Reverend Dr. LeRoy Attles, Sr.

A man of God, and the husband I have grown to love more and more with the passing of each year that God has blessed us to spend together.

Contents

List Of Tables

List Of Figures

Preface

This book is a study to evaluate the impact that changes in living environments (i.e., from homelessness, in a shelter unit, to the family's own dwelling unit) have on the academic achievement of school-age children.

The study samples seven cases of public school children who were in grades 5 through 8, during the years 1988 to 1991. It compares the academic achievement scores of these children on the same standardized test during two points in their education: when they lived in a sheltered unit and when they returned to the family's own dwelling. The researcher hypothesized that homelessness adversely influences academic achievement in eight academic categories. The academic categories, as defined by the California Achievement Test, are: Word Analysis, Vocabulary, Comprehension, Spelling, Language Mechanics, Language Expression, Mathematics Computation, and Mathematics Concepts and Application. The case study technique is used along with pattern-matching (i.e., quasi-experimental) research methodology to compare and measure the achievement of children during the period in which they were classified as homeless.

This study matched the academic achievement score to the norm academic achievement score in order to determine the impact of the homeless experience on each category listed on the California Achievement Test Battery. There were two possible outcomes for academic achievement–a positive performance or a negative performance. All scores over the district mean in each of the categories resulted in a positive, or increase in, performance and the conclusion that homelessness has "no effect" on academic achievement. Scores below the district mean for each of the categories resulted in negative, or decrease in, performance and the conclusion that homelessness has "an effect" on academic achievement.

The results of the study indicate that homelessness has an adverse effect on the academic achievement of school-age children. The study also suggests that if supportive educational services are not received while the school-age child is homeless, when he/she returns to living within a family unit, his/her academic achievement results on the standardized California Achievement Test would tend to show a negative deviation from the district mean.

Acknowledgments

Without the care, support, encouragement, guidance, and prayers from my family; the Rev. Dr. LeRoy Attles; Sr. Rev. Kanice and Timothy Johns; Mr. & Mrs. LeRoy Attles, Jr.; Rev. Louis Attles; and grandchildren; Mark, Genice, Kara and Joy; and the members of my University of Massachusetts dissertation committee: Dr. Robert R. Wellman who served as Chair and Dr. Atron A. Gentry and Dr. Edgar E. Smith for their insightful comments and supportive feedback, the completion of this document would not have been a possibility.

The Effects of Homelessness on the Academic Achievement of Children

I

Introduction

> Men make their own history, but they do not make it just as
> they please; they do not make it under circumstances chosen
> by themselves but under circumstances directly encountered,
> given and transmitted from the past.   – Karl Marx
> *Eighteenth Brumaire*

The above quotation emphasizes the significance of supportive
environments to the productivity and intellectual development of the
individual. It is also indicative of the projections that uneducated or
undereducated youth can expect to be unemployed or underpaid and
thus live unproductive lives, accumulate very little material wealth,
and ultimately be forced to live in substandard housing or no housing
at all. Evidence indicates that the United States is a society where
millions of people are transient and/or homeless. One of the
increasingly visible and growing sub–populations of the homeless is
families with children (Coalition for the Homeless, 1984). The
primary cause of homelessness is poverty. Poverty is directly and
positively correlated with unemployment and underemployment and
correlates with the lack of adequate education. In view of the
importance of education as a fundamental means of changing life
cycles and its direct relationship to income and employment, this
study will undertake to answer the following question: "Does a change
in living environment from family unit to shelter unit have an effect
on the academic performance of school–age children who have
become homeless?"

This research question will be approached by examining and
comparing yearly academic achievement scores in the categories of
Word Analysis, Vocabulary, Comprehension, Spelling, Language
Mechanics, Language Expression, Mathematics Computation, and
Mathematics Concepts and Application.

Academic achievement will be measured by using the pattern–matched pair methodology to identify the impact that changes in living environments from the families' own dwelling units to sheltered units have on the academic achievement of school–age children who are homeless. These scores will be pattern–matched twice. They will be matched for the identical categories and compared once during the period in which the child was homeless and again after they are returned to a family unit living environment. All the scores will then be pattern–matched with the school district's norms for scores attained on the California Achievement Test in like categories to determine the effect of homelessness.

This study will examine the relationship between academic achievement and homelessness using the seven cases of school–age children living in an urban transitional shelter.

STATEMENT OF THE PROBLEM

The homeless transient, the wandering loner who may be alcoholic or mentally disabled, is no longer typical of the great majority of people who are without shelter. More and more, those sleeping in emergency shelters include parents and children whose primary reason for homelessness is poverty and some other emergent which causes family disruption and is directly related to the disruption of the education process.

In light of the increasing number of children who are living in transitional environments, the problem is to determine the impact of homelessness on the academic achievement of the school–age child. This study will also focus on identifying specific resources needed to assist the children in overcoming educational deficiencies and to proceed to become productive citizens.

The number of homeless individuals is growing geometrically. Not only are there more homeless people in urban areas and throughout the United States than at any time since the Great Depression of 1929, homelessness is now more racially and sexually diverse, expands over generations, and includes people and families who are, in most respects, like other poor people, except that they cannot find or afford housing.

Homeless youth represent the fastest growing subgroup of homeless people in the United States. The 1988 national estimates of the population of children who are homeless ranged from 350,000 to 500,000. The majority of these children and adolescents are not runaways, but either live with their families or have been abandoned, abused, or released from foster care, with no resources for independent living.

In addition, a count of the actual number of homeless is difficult to obtain because the most carefully compiled statistics are probably incomplete and unreliable. There is a tendency, in rural regions, to report that little or no homelessness exists, in part because the lack of available services drive the rural homeless out of their home counties to cities where shelters exist, and in part because of the invisibility of people living in abandoned barns, chicken coops, cars, in the woods, etc.

Even in urban areas where facilities are more likely to exist, it is difficult to obtain accurate figures. Many more people are turned away from shelters than can be accommodated. Therefore, substantially greater numbers of people end up sleeping on the streets and in other public places than sleeping in shelters, according to several reputable studies. Many homeless youngsters sleep on benches in bus terminals, train stations, parks, telephone booths, or in all–night restaurants. Many homeless youngsters attempt to find secluded refuges where they can stay out of sight in order to avoid eviction by police. Abandoned buildings, dark basements and hallways, steam tunnels, empty garages, and the bathrooms of deserted public places offer not only shelter from the elements, but some degree of privacy and safety.

Studies also show that the homeless population is becoming younger. Data aggregated for the United States reveal that young single adults (under 30 years of age) and families presently account for approximately 50 to 75 percent of the homeless people seeking services. These statistics do not include the great number of young people living on the brink of eviction, or those who have already doubled up with friends or relatives for shelter, unable to afford places of their own. On October 8, 1988, *The Washington Post* reported that more than one–third of single–parent families spend 75 percent or more of their income for rent. For Black women, who head more than one–half of all Black families, the burden can be even heavier. Any unexpected crisis can push many low–income women over the edge into poverty and homelessness. Single women face the worst difficulties. Their numbers have grown from 10 percent of the homeless in some states to 25 percent over a few years.

PURPOSE OF THE STUDY

The purpose of this study is to examine and compare yearly academic achievement scores and to identify the impact that the change in living environment from shelter unit to family unit has on the academic achievement of school–age children.

To achieve this objective, the study will examine seven cases of school–age children who lived in a transitional shelter homeless environment and in a family environment. The specific categories of each case to be examined on the California Achievement Test are: Word Analysis, Vocabulary, Comprehension, Spelling, Language Mechanics, Language Expression, Mathematics Computation, and Mathematics Concepts and Application. These categories are matched to the California Achievement Test scores when the school–age children were homeless and when they were returned to a family unit. All achievement scores of the seven cases will then be matched with the school district's score on the California Achievement Test in the same categories to estimate the variance and to determine the effect of homelessness on the academic achievement of school–age children.

These seven cases of homeless students (independent variables) have been exposed to the specific condition of homelessness (i.e., school–age children living in transitional housing). Their academic achievement (dependent variables) will be compared to the academic achievement of the average student not exposed to the condition of homelessness, in order to test the hypothesis that homelessness adversely affects academic achievement.

The study will use the test scores of seven case studies for eight California Achievement Test categories and will compare the achievement of homeless children with the norm school district scores. The achievements of the sample group (homeless children) are compared to achievements of children of the same age and grade who are controlled for the same cognitive ability but differ in the fact that the sample group lived in a family shelter when the California Achievement Battery Test was first examined and had been returned to a family dwelling unit when the same battery of tests were administered a year later.

HYPOTHESIS

It is hypothesized that the academic achievement of school–age children is negatively influenced by the condition of homelessness. When school–age children do not experience the condition of homelessness, their academic achievement scores on eight education categories of the California Achievement Test will tend to fluctuate around the norm range for the school district. However, when school–age children are homeless, their standard academic achievement scores will tend to significantly vary from the norm of the school district test scores in the eight categories measured by the California Achievement Test (Word Analysis, Vocabulary, Comprehension, Spelling, Language Mechanics, Language Expression, Mathematics Computation, and Mathematics Concepts and Application).

SIGNIFICANCE OF THE STUDY

There are several benefits to undertaking this study. First, the results will discover if academic achievement diminishes when children become homeless. If the results show diminished academic achievement, as hypothesized, the results will contribute to heightening the awareness of the areas and type of academic support needed by school–age children who are homeless.

The results of this study can also be used by shelter providers as the impetus necessary for hiring tutors, resource teachers, workshop leaders, and other specific resource personnel to meet the educational program goals as requested by the Department of Health and Human Services in their shelter proposals.

The ultimate goal of this study is to provide the motivation for continued research on the subject of homelessness and academic achievement, to support school age children who are homeless with achievement support services, and to interrupt the potential cycle of intergenerational homelessness.

This study will be useful in systematizing the academic achievement status of school–age homeless children and in providing a more solid research knowledge base on which to design and implement future programs for homeless school–age children.

This study will also be useful in collaborating findings which suggest that homeless school–age children need an individual education plan developed and implemented specifically to the needs of the child who has been homeless.

DELIMITATIONS OF THE STUDY

This study is limited to an examination of seven cases reviewed at the Central Office of the School Department. Children identified as homeless have met the condition of having lived in the transitional house during the school years investigated in this study (1988–1989, 1989–1990, and 1990–1991). Children were in grades 5 to 8, where a complete battery of tests were given on the categories of Word Analysis, Vocabulary, Comprehension, Spelling, Language Mechanics, Language Expression, Mathematics Computation, and Mathematics Concepts and Application, to determine the total academic achievement level as measured by the California Achievement Test.

The children who are under investigation within this research study lived in the same transitional house while they were homeless and attended the same urban school system. The children had taken the complete battery of standardized California Achievement Tests while they were homeless and the next year when they were no longer homeless.

The condition of sheltered environments may not be typical across the country. Therefore, these findings may not be generalized to all homeless children.

DEFINITION OF TERMS

The following glossary of terms was developed to insure the readers' understanding of the way in which terms were used throughout the study.

Clients: For the purpose of this study, any persons who have been referred by the Department of Health and Human Services and are living in a transitional house.

Comprehension: As used in the California Achievement Test, the test questions that measure comprehension of reading passages, test the student's ability to extract details, analyze characters, identify main ideas, and interpret events described in passages.

Family Emergency Shelter or a Transitional House: A designated facility which has as its primary goal to ensure the immediate safety of homeless families by providing temporary shelter and meals or access to kitchen facilities to prepare meals.

Homeless: As defined in Section 103(a) of the McKinney Act, (1) an individual who lacks a fixed, regular, and adequate nighttime residence; and (2) an individual who has a primary nighttime residence that is (a) a supervised publicly or privately operated shelter designed to provide temporary living accommodations (including welfare hotels, congregate shelters, and transitional housing for the mentally ill); (b) an institution that provides a temporary residence for individuals intended to be institutionalized; or (c) a public or private place not designed for, or ordinarily used as, a regular sleeping accommodation for human beings. Section 103(c) excludes from the definition of homeless "any individual imprisoned or otherwise detained pursuant to an Act of Congress or a State law." Certain categories of individuals easily fall within this definition. For example, homeless children would include those living in welfare motels and transitional housing shelters, as well as those who sleep in the streets, in cars, or in abandoned buildings because they lack regular access to adequate housing.

Homeless School–Age Child: Any child residing or living in a transitory shelter, who is of school–age and whose parents have met the legally defined admission criteria for "homeless".

Language Expression: As used in the California Achievement Test, the test questions that measure skills in language usage and sentence structure. Items require identification of the correct noun, pronoun, verb, or adjective that completes a sentence. Other items require identification of correct sentence structure, including substitution of the correct pronoun for nouns in a sentence and changing a statement to a question. All items in the test are based on rules of written standard English.

Language Mechanics: As used in the California Achievement Test, the test questions that measure skills in the mechanics of capitalization and punctuation.

LEAs: Local education agencies (i.e., a city school system).

Mathematics Computation: As used in the California Achievement Test, the test questions that measure computation skills in the addition and subtraction of whole numbers.

Mathematics Concepts and Application: As used in the California Achievement Test, the test questions that measure understanding of mathematical concepts. Specific skills include concepts dealing with numeration, problem solving, measurement, and geometry.

SEAs: State education agencies (i.e., State Department of Education).

Spelling: As used in the California Achievement Test, the test questions that measure application of spelling rules for consonants, vowels, and various structural forms. Items are presented in the context of sentences with a missing word. The student identifies the correct spelling of the word to complete the sentence.

Vocabulary: As used in the California Achievement Test, the test questions which measure the same–meaning words, opposite–meaning words, and words in context.

Word Analysis: As used in the California Achievement Test, the test questions which measure understanding of structural word parts and word forms. The student identifies initial or final cluster and digraph sounds, vowel sounds, and diphthongs or variant vowel sounds. Also measured are recognition of sight words, inflectional endings, and compound words.

TECHNIQUE AND RESEARCH METHODOLOGY

This study uses the case study technique to gather data as it is applicable to the method used to gather and store information related to homelessness. The study employs the pattern–matching methodology. Pattern matching is a quasi form of the experimental research methodology. Matched pair, matched designs, or pattern match are all terms for the quasi–experimental research method which is aimed at investigating possible cause–and–effect relationships by comparing a group's behavior to the controlled behavior (Cook & Campbell, 1979).

The child's achievement will be compared and evaluated using the school district California Achievement Test scores as the mean or norm.

The pattern–matching approach to social research is strongly related to the developing process of construct validity which has occurred over the past thirty years and is attributed to Cronbach and

Meehl (1955), Campbell and Stanley (1963), Campbell and Fiske (1959), and Cook and Campbell (1979). According to Campbell (1975), quasi–experimental research proposes to approximate the conditions of the true experiment in a setting which does not allow the control and/or manipulation of all relevant variables.

Construct validity refers to the degree to which observations can be said to reflect their theoretical constructs. Construct validity depends on the matching and comparing of patterns of occurrences. For example, in order to establish that a measure reflects conditions it is supposed to reflect, the following are needed: (1) a conceptualization or theory of the expected relationships between the variable of interest and related variables from which they must be distinguished (the conceptualization pattern); (2) observed interdependencies between purported measures of the variable of interest and related variables (the operational pattern); and (3) a "match" between these two patterns (Trochim, 1985).

The conceptual pattern for the study is that homelessness has an adverse impact on the academic achievement of school–age children. The homeless child will fall below the norm of the academic achievement scores of children without the experience of homelessness. In addition, this study will match the academic achievement score to the norm academic achievement score in order to determine the impact of the homeless experience on each category of the California Achievement Test (Word Analysis, Vocabulary, Comprehension, Spelling, Language Mechanics, Language Expression, Mathematics Computation, and Mathematics Concepts and Application).

The operational pattern for this study (i.e., the independent variable) is the scores of the academic achievement observed in each of the categories of the California Achievement Test as related to the norm for that grade. A match between these patterns for the study will be the analysis of the independent and dependent variables.

In this research study, there are two possible outcomes for academic achievement–a positive performance and a negative performance. All scores over the district mean in each of the categories will result in a positive, or increase in, performance and lead to the conclusion that homelessness has "no effect" on academic achievement. Scores below the district mean for each of the categories will result in a negative, or decrease in, performance and lead to the conclusion that homelessness has "an effect" on academic achievement.

OUTLINE OF THE CHAPTERS

The first chapter highlights the problem, its nature, scope and significance. It introduces a general description of the case study technique, pattern–matching methodology, and the quasi–experimental research design strategy to be used to collect, examine, analyze, and evaluate the data included in this study.

Chapter 2 presents the literature review. It provides references to published contributions on the national subject of homelessness, homelessness of children, the effects of homelessness on school–age children, and the impact which homelessness has on the educational achievement of children.

The case study technique and the pattern–matching (quasi–experimental) research methodology of the study is discussed in Chapter 3.

Case study data are presented in Chapter 4. This chapter also analyzes and evaluates the impact of homelessness upon the academic achievement of school–age children. It reports and compares descriptive data of the academic achievement scores of children during a period of homelessness and a year later, when these same children were living in a family dwelling unit. The patternmatching methodology is used to analyze the relationship of the academic achievement scores of children who have had a homeless experience (during the period of homelessness and the year preceding homelessness) with the norm scores of children who have not had the homeless experience to determine the impact of the experience upon academic achievement.

Chapter 5 is devoted to the summary, conclusions, and recommendations resulting from the data analysis.

Further discussion on the issue of homelessness and selected innovative programs are presented in Chapter 6.

II

Review Of The Literature

Homelessness is a national problem which has political, socioeconomic, psychological, and educational implications for a person's well–being in this society. The resulting effect of these multifaceted implications, varied circumstances, and characteristics of the homeless have the potential of threatening the nation's productivity and representing a tragic waste of children's lives.

Having said this, the goal of this review of literature is to explore in depth the political, socioeconomic, psychological, and educational factors impacting homelessness. The review is essentially undertaken in four sections. Section one examines the political factors influencing homelessness and its effect on the academic achievement of school–age children. Section two examines the socioeconomic factors influencing homelessness and its effect on the academic achievement of school–age children. Section three examines the psychological factors influencing the homeless and its effect on the academic achievement of school–age children. Section four examines the educational factors influencing homelessness and its effect on the academic achievement of school–age children.

POLITICAL IMPLICATIONS OF HOMELESSNESS

In July of 1987, Congress passed the Stewart B. McKinney Homeless Assistance Act (P.L. 100–77), the first piece of comprehensive national legislation addressing the problem of homelessness.

Recognizing the needs of the 14 million people who are the at–risk population, and the benefits of assisting these people before they become homeless, Congress placed emphasis on homelessness prevention activities when it passed the Stewart B. McKinney Homeless Assistance Amendments Act of 1988 (P.L. 100–629) on November 7, 1988, and the McKinney Act (P.L. 100–77) on July 22,

1987, and its amendments. These make up the first comprehensive homeless assistance law, creating a wide range of programs and benefits. They defined the goal of state and local governments and local homeless assistance providers as being responsible for the various programs to keep people from becoming homeless. As part of the act, states are now required to ensure that homeless children are guaranteed access to education. Grant funds were made available to assess the needs of homeless children in each state, and to designate a state coordinator to assist in the design and implementation of programs.

Some programs provide financial assistance, such as payments for rent, security deposits, mortgages, and heating bills. Others provide services, such as legal aid, landlord–tenant mediation, budget counseling, and referrals to other assistance programs. Many assistance providers believe that the case management approach was the most effective way to provide assistance to those at risk of homelessness. This approach includes assessing an individual's particular needs, providing a combination of financial and other assistance, and following up on that person's progress in maintaining his or her home.

Six federal programs provided an important source of funds for many of these homeless prevention activities. Three of these are administered by the Department of Health and Human Services (HHS), two by the Department of Housing and Urban Development (HUD), and one by the Federal Emergency Management Agency (FEMA). Together, these programs made available at least 320 million dollars in fiscal year 1989 to state and local organizations.

The Stewart B. McKinney Homeless Assistance Act (P.L. 100–77) requires that each state educational agency (SEA) ensure each homeless family and youth access to a free and appropriate education. Under the Act, SEAs are to gather data on the number and location of homeless children and youth in their state and develop a state plan for meeting the Federal Government guidelines. In addition, SEAs are to collaborate with local government agencies (LEAs) in designing and implementing local programs which are consistent with their state plans. The political effect of homelessness, according to the requirements of this law, is to ensure access to a free and appropriate education. For each homeless school–age child, this law suggests that homeless children who are not progressing academically are children who are not receiving an appropriate education as mandated by the Stewart B. McKinney Homeless Assistance Act (P.L. 100–77). Therefore, one of the reasons this study is significant is that it will focus on "the intellectual changes in the scores of homeless school–age elementary children as reflected by their academic achievement on their annual California Achievement Test scores."

SOCIOECONOMIC IMPLICATIONS OF HOMELESSNESS

The socioeconomic implications of homelessness are identified by conditions such as increases in population, decline in student school attendance, poor health care, and decline in the standard of living. The socioeconomic influences have become more prevalent because of the growing visibility of the homeless on our streets, in our public facilities, and in the media. Researchers, such as Bassuk (1985), and Eddowes and Hranity (1989), estimate the growing homeless population to range in numbers anywhere from 250 thousand to 3 million. Wells (1990) suggests that an even greater number may be at risk of becoming homeless. For example, according to one recent study, Bowen et al. (1989) estimate that as many as 14 million families are currently in danger of losing their homes because of eviction and/or mortgage foreclosure. Included in these disturbing statistics are homeless families with children, the fastest growing segment of this population. In agreement is the Missouri Department of Education predictions that the homeless population will increase 10 to 30 percent each year and that more children face the possibility of growing up in shelters or on the streets (Bowen et al., 1989).

The socioeconomic implications are seen in the increasing numbers of school–age children who are not attending school. Rafferty and Rollins (1989) suggest that 57 percent of school–age children are not attending school on a regular basis.

Other data highlighting the depth of this crisis includes a U. S. Department of Education (1989) report to Congress, which estimates that there are 220,000 school–age homeless children nationwide. Approximately 65,000, or 30 percent, of these children are not regularly attending school (U. S. Department of Education, 1989). The figures from the Coalition for the Homeless (1984) are even more startling. This group concludes that there are between 500,000 and 750,000 school–age children who are homeless.

The socioeconomic influences are seen in the definitions of homelessness and the descriptions of the places used as shelters. The characteristics of homelessness deal with two dimensions–place and time. With regard to place, some consider the homeless only to be those who sleep either in emergency shelters or in places not usually used as a home, such as cars, abandoned buildings, subways, bus and train terminals, steam grates or doorways, beaches, caves, woods, tents, or park benches. Others extend the list to include the homes of others (often friends or relatives) or flophouses, single room occupancy (SRO) hotels, jails, detoxification centers, and migrant worker housing. With regard to time, some consider homelessness to include those sleeping in unconventional or temporary surroundings for brief periods in the wake of a disaster or eviction, while others at least implicitly define homelessness as a long–term phenomenon affecting a much smaller number. The problem of "homelessness" looks very different depending on how tightly the boundaries of time and place are drawn.

A narrow definition conveys the impression that relatively few people are seriously deprived of shelter and understates the extent to which certain kinds of people are thus deprived. A broader definition may blur the distinction between homelessness and the larger problems of distinction between homelessness and poverty. Some definitions used in recent studies of the problem are listed below. There is no correct definition; rather, the following are definitions used by various organizations:

- The Alcohol, Drug Abuse, and Mental Health Administration (ADAMHA) has developed this working definition: A homeless person is "anyone who lacks adequate shelter, resources, and community ties" (Levin, 1984).
- The Department of Housing and Urban Development (HUD) classified a person as homeless if he or she slept (1) in public or private emergency shelters which take a variety of forms– armories, schools, church basements, government buildings, former firehouses, and where temporary vouchers are provided by private and public agencies, even hotels, apartments, or boarding homes, or (2) in the streets, parks, subways, bus terminals, railroad stations, airports, under bridges or aqueducts, in

abandoned buildings without utilities, cars, trucks, or any of the public or private space that is not designed for shelter.

- The National Institute of Mental Health (NIMH) proposed a far broader, but vague, definition of homelessness, not entirely based on type of shelter: "Anyone who lacks adequate shelter, resources, and community ties."

- The Community Services Society of New York (a non–profit human service organization) added to the NIMH definition: "Those whose primary residence is in other well–hidden sites known only to their users."

- The U. S. General Accounting Office (1990) uses a definition that encompasses the common components of the above definitions to include: "Those persons who lack resources and community ties necessary to provide for their own adequate shelter."

- The Ohio Department of Mental Health was more specific in its definition, suggesting that those living in extremely substandard housing, such as flophouses or single–room only (SRO) hotels, are homeless if they only have sufficient resources to reside in these places for less than 45 days and consider themselves to be homeless. In addition, the Ohio definition includes those who have been forced to move in with friends and relatives on a temporary basis (also 45 days or less) because they have become homeless.

The Department of Housing and Urban Development (HUD) definition is useful for measuring the current level of need for emergency shelters and related services. The Ohio study definition, which is broader than HUD's in terms of place, is perhaps more useful for exploratory research on the nature and causes of homelessness. Casting a broader net permits a more extensive set of comparisons.

"Under all definitions, homelessness refers not to an absolute condition but to a deprivation that varies in degree, depending on the extent to which the location is temporary or unstable, and the length of time these conditions must be endured" (Redburn & Terry, 1986). Further, Section 103(a) of the McKinney Act (1988) defines the term "homeless" as including:

1. An individual who lacks a fixed, regular, and adequate nighttime residence; and

2. An individual who has a primary nighttime residence that is:

    - a supervised publicly or privately operated shelter designed to provide temporary living accommodations (including welfare hotels, congregate shelters, and transitional housing for the mentally ill);
    - an institution that provides a temporary residence for individuals intended to be institutionalized; or
    - a public or private place not designed for, or ordinarily used as, a regular sleeping accommodation for human beings.

Section 103(c) excludes from the definition of homeless "any individual imprisoned or otherwise detained pursuant to an Act of Congress or a state law."

Certain categories of individuals easily fall within this definition. For example, homeless children would include those living in welfare motels and transitional housing shelters, as well as those who sleep in the streets, in cars, or in abandoned buildings because they lack regular access to adequate housing.

The following demographics described by the Human Resources Administration of New York City (HRANYC) are cited by Wilson (1989) and by Redburn and Terry (1986). In January of 1985, a longitudinal study was conducted of 196 families tracked for a six–month period. The families were most often headed by single, unemployed females in their late twenties, who dropped out of high school and had three or four children. Almost two–thirds had lost their apartments because of a fire or a vacate order. Over 20 percent were evicted by a primary tenant with whom the family had stayed for at least three months, and long–term housing could not be provided due to overcrowding and family conflicts. The average family moved three times before becoming homeless (Human Resources Administration of New York City, 1985).

Wilson (1989) describes the demographics of the homeless as young persons often in their twenties or thirties, who may have children and some have jobs. They are homeless due to a fire, a job loss, an abusive spouse, or a rent increase. In Wilson's (1989) description of the homeless, he outlines the following statistics as a Homeless Family index:

- There are more than 500,000 homeless children in the United States.
- 43 percent of homeless children do not attend school.
- The number of homeless families in the United States will rise by 25 percent this year.
- Eviction and spiraling rents displace 2.5 million people from their homes each year.
- 750,000 new low–income housing units are needed each year to house the homeless.
- 13.8 million children are living in poverty.
- 15 percent of American children are born into poverty.

SHELTERS AND WELFARE HOTELS

The characteristics of homelessness describe the kind of places homeless people live. One of the places they might stay in is a shelter which is usually located in the most dangerous sections of the city (Bassuk, 1987). For example, at the Pine Street Inn, the largest shelter in Boston (Massachusetts), it is not uncommon for guests to be assaulted, raped, or robbed on the premises. In addition to the element of danger, shelters often have little or no privacy for guests, with large rooms containing row after row of cots with no more than three feet between each, and no curtain partitions or other ways to separate the 50 or more people occupying the same room (Mowbray, 1985). Another place where the homeless live is in Welfare Hotels, which are considered the next step from the congregate shelter. Typically, they are located in filthy, dangerous areas that are inappropriate for raising children. Many of the hotels are found in centers of pornography, drug trafficking, and prostitution. The average family stays about one year. This is a figure that does not always take into account time already spent in the shelters. The hotels are paid an average of $1,800 per month to shelter a family of four in a single room without kitchen facilities (Herbert, 1985).

Pressed for a solution, some cities warehouse families in motels or hotels. In *Rachel and Her Children*, Kozol (1988) describes life in the Martinique, the largest of these hotels in New York City: "It is difficult to do justice to the sense of hopelessness one feels on entering the building. Something of Dickens' halls of chancery comes to mind." He tells about a large population of cockroaches and rodents, elevators that do not work, drugs, violence (including murder), theft, prostitution, trash filled halls, and broken plumbing. Families of four or five crowd into one room with several beds and not enough chairs. They get a restaurant allowance, but Kozol notes: "It is intended to buy groceries. They cannot cook in kitchens they don't have, and must therefore try somehow to cook on hot plates that they are not officially permitted to possess. If they use the restaurant, their children will soon starve. If they cook within their rooms, they break a rule to which they have agreed. If they are discovered in infraction of a rule, they are at the mercy of the guard who discovered their offense." New York City pays the owner of this and other hotels about $60 per night for a room for a family. *The New York Times* estimates the City spends about $70,000 a year on each homeless family.

Washington, D. C. has what some call an open–market system. Homeless families report to the Pitts each day where the city feeds them and assigns them a shelter for the night. One of these is a converted gymnasium, the outside of which has a bleak, jail–like appearance. Inside, the stench of urine floods the room, which is divided like a stable by plywood partitions. Each stall has a sheet in front of the entrance and army cots and blankets inside. Families use common bathing facilities, and savvy parents accompany their children to the toilet (Wilson, 1989).

In summary, the breakdown in the family structure, the unavailable affordable housing, inadequate welfare benefits, insufficient medical care, and teen pregnancy are considered contributory socioeconomic factors in the growing national tragedy of homelessness. Each of these factors could have an effect upon the academic achievement of school–age children and each of these will put them at risk of dropping out of school.

Although socioeconomic homeless conditions vary from state to state, several factors are generally recognized as contributing to homelessness. Those factors most frequently mentioned by providers of emergency services are:

1. A shortage of affordable housing (e.g., cutbacks in housing subsidies).

2. Increased unemployment (*Scientific America*, July, 1984; *The Washington Post Magazine*, May 29, 1988).

3. Low public assistance payments (including cutbacks in unemployment assistance).

4. The break–up of families.

5. Eviction for failure to meet rent and mortgage payments.

6. Parents may also place children in foster care to protect them from the hardships of homelessness. Unfortunately, this often only postpones the problem. Many homeless youth tend to be former foster children who have come of age and left home without skills or other preparation for independent living.

7. Domestic violence. (There are thousands of women in battered women's facilities. Many of these women have their children with them or they are homeless because these shelters cannot accommodate these families.)

8. Chronic mental illness.

9. De–institutionalization of homeless people.

Elementary school–age children in grades 5 through 8, homeless as a result of these determinants, are the focus of this study. The researcher hypothesizes that homelessness adversely influences academic achievement as measured by standardized test scores. Therefore, the study will concentrate on changes in the academic achievement of elementary children living in a family shelter in an urban environment.

PSYCHOLOGICAL IMPLICATIONS OF HOMELESSNESS

From the time a child becomes homeless, the effects of poverty–removal from a familiar environment, irregularity of eating and poor nourishment, poor access to public health care, and residential crowding with unhealthy conditions have already begun to show. There is a high incidence of hypertension, respiratory infection, alcohol and narcotic abuse (New York State Department of Social Services, 1984). The younger the children are, the more likely that they will regress developmentally (Kilman, 1986).

Residents living in two shelters and eight hotels for homeless families reported an increase in children's acting–out behavior with concurrent fighting and restlessness. Next in frequency were periods of depression, moodiness, and low frustration tolerance. Teachers also reported an increase in these problems.

The research of Bassuk (1985) concludes that homeless preschoolers manifested multiple severe developmental lags, while the homeless school–age children were so anxious and depressed that many had to repeat a grade.

Another factor causing homelessness is that many of the homeless families have been victims of fire. Therefore, professionals working with this population should be sensitized to related issues. Krim (1982) summarized common reactions experienced by families after fire: withdrawal and isolation of adults from their children, disorientation and confusion, grieving over loss of possessions, family disorganization, and confusion, break–up, aggressive reactions, sleep disorders, and psychosomatic complaints. Homeless children, however, project one or more of the aforementioned symptoms related to a feeling of loss even though they may not have experienced a fire. Moving strains the concept of self and world with children. Baster (1985) describes another desperate need, which is to provide the opportunity for recreational outlets. From the limited research completed on the plight of homeless school–age children and youth, Frawley and Zafonte (1984) have described the general problems which exist: First, homeless children have multiple needs requiring a broad range of integrated services. Second, although they have certain problems in common with all homeless persons, they also have special problems directly related to their developmental needs. Third, the few programs currently serving homeless families with school–age children focus on the immediate crises of homelessness and not on the longer term needs of these youth.

In summation, one of the most important procedures in working with these multi–traumatized children is to first understand the conditions in which they live and the psychological effects these living conditions could have on them. The examination of the California Achievement Test scores will bring awareness of the supportive services needed to maintain the academic achievement of homeless school–age children while they are homeless. Proper supportive services could eliminate failure to make their grade and alleviate many of the psychological effects of homelessness.

EDUCATIONAL IMPLICATIONS OF HOMELESSNESS

The complexity of access, placement, transportation, and instructional issues involved in educating the homeless school–age population underscores the significant challenges confronting the Educational System. Because homeless children and youth, by definition, lack permanent shelter and typically have limited access to adequate clothing, nutrition, and health services, their capacity to benefit from schooling is often impaired. It is clear, therefore, that providing an appropriate education to homeless children and youth–is a significant state education agency (SEA) and local education agency (LEA) responsibility–one which must involve collaboration with other community organizations actively providing services to homeless families and individuals (Policy Study Association, Inc., 1990). All community organizations providing services to homeless families and the educational systems must work together. The research conducted by Bassuk (1985) suggested that most school–age homeless children become anxious and so depressed that they end up repeating a grade. The investigation conducted by Wells (1990) included a description of the most frequently listed problems of homeless children as cited by their parents. Each issue on the following list has educational implications for disruption of academic achievement and could cause a homeless student to repeat a grade:

- Transporting homeless students, many of whom change shelters often.

- School records are rarely intact. Homeless children may end up having to be re–immunized.

- As students move from school to school, the teachers do not have enough time to assess their needs.

- Homeless students rarely have space or peace and quiet for homework. Shelters are often large, noisy rooms that are shared with their entire family.

- Education is not a priority of homeless families, as parents are preoccupied with finding food, safe shelter, and employment.
- There is a general lack of community services for homeless families, including health and mental health care for school–age mothers.

In the classroom, the task of a teacher working with a homeless child is to provide a structured, stable, non–threatening environment. For young children, this could mean giving children cubbies with their names and defining personal boundaries. Geivertzman and Fodor (1987) and Coles (1976) are in agreement that rootless children may leave tasks unfinished. Therefore, teachers should assign projects that can be broken down into small, manageable segments which the children can handle with success.

III

Methodology Of The Study

The major objective of this research study is to investigate whether or not academic achievement diminishes when children become homeless. The results will contribute to heightening the awareness that increased academic support is needed by school–age children who are homeless.

This study used the case study technique to gather data related to homelessness. It used the components of case study techniques as described by Cronbach et al. (1980), Guba and Lincoln (1981), Jacobs (1970), Patton (1980), and Yin (1984). They agree that the most important applications of the case study technique are to explain the causal links in real life interventions, describe the real–life context in which an intervention has occurred, and explore those situations in which the intervention being evaluated has no clear, single set of outcomes.

The intent of this study was to examine the causal links of homelessness to the academic achievement of seven homeless school–age children in the categories listed on the standardized California Achievement Test (Word Analysis, Vocabulary, Comprehension, Spelling, Language Mechanics, Language Expression, Mathematics Computation, and Mathematics Concepts and Application). The case study technique is a preferred strategy when the investigator has little control over events and when the focus is a contemporary phenomenon within some real–life contact (Yin, 1984).

The case study technique also was used because, like experiments, case studies are generalized to theoretical propositions rather than to a population or to a universe. One approach for linking data to a proposition for case studies is the method of "pattern–matching," employed in this study. Pattern–matching is a quasi–experimental form of research methodology. Matched pair, matched design, or pattern match are all terms for this quasi–experimental research method which is aimed at investigating possible cause–and–effect relationships by comparing group behavior (Cook & Campbell, 1979). Campbell (1975) describes the pattern–matching methodology as one in which several pieces of information from the same case may be related to some theoretical proposition. He indicated two potential propositions and showed that the data matched one better than the other. If the two potential patterns are considered rival propositions, one is considered as "an effect" and the other is considered as "no effect." The pattern–matching methodology is the process of relating the data to the proposition. The analytic methodology of pattern–matching was used to address internal validity. This study tried to determine if event "X" (homelessness) has a significant impact on event "Y" (diminished academic achievement). The results will be extended to make inferences.

The pattern–matching approach to social research is strongly related to the developing process of construct validity which has occurred over the past thirty years and is attributed to Campbell and Fiske (1959), Campbell and Stanley (1963), Cook and Campbell (1979), and Cronbach and Meehl (1955). In accordance with Campbell (1975), quasi–experimental research proposes to approximate the conditions of the true experiment in a setting which does not allow the control and/or manipulation of all relevant variables.

Construct validity refers to the degree to which observations can be said to reflect their theoretical constructs. Construct validity depends on the matching and comparing of patterns of occurrences. In order to establish that a measure reflects conditions it is supposed to reflect, the following are needed: (1) a conceptualization or theory of the expected relationships between the variables of interest and related variables from which they must be distinguished (the conceptualization pattern); (2) observed interdependencies between purported measures of the variable of interest and related variables (the operational pattern); and (3) a "match" between these two patterns (Trochim, 1985).

The conceptual pattern for the study is that homelessness has an impact on the academic achievement of school–age children. Because of the experience of homelessness, the homeless child achievement scores tend to fall below the norm of the academic achievement scores of children who have not had the experience of homelessness. In addition, this study matches the academic achievement score to the norm academic achievement score in order to determine the impact of the homeless experience on each category listed on the California Achievement Test (Word Analysis, Vocabulary, Comprehension, Spelling, Language Mechanisms, Language Expression, Mathematics Computation, and Mathematics Concepts and Application). The operational pattern for this study (i.e., the independent variable) is the scores of the categories of the California Achievement Test as related to the norm for that grade. A match between these patterns for the study was the analysis of the independent and dependent variables.

In this study, there are two possible outcomes for academic achievement–a positive performance or a negative performance. All scores above the district mean in each of the categories will result in a positive, or increase in, performance with the conclusion that homelessness has "no effect" on academic achievement. Scores below the district mean for each of the categories will result in a negative, or decrease in, performance with the conclusion that homelessness has "an effect" on academic achievement.

INSTRUMENT

The instrument used for testing was the California Achievement Test, Forms E and F (CAT E and F), published by McGraw Hill in 1985. This series of tests is designed to measure achievement in the basic skills commonly found in state and district curricula. They provide information about the relative ranking of students against a norm group (a pattern regarded as typical for a specific group), as well as specific information about the instructional needs of students. The basic subject areas measured by the California Achievement Test, Forms E and F. are Reading, Spelling, Language, Mathematics, and Study Skills. During the Fall of 1984 and the Spring of 1985, the California Achievement Test, Forms E and F. were tested for standardization. The tests were administered to a large nationwide sample of grades K through 12. The public school sample was stratified by geographic region, communities (urban, suburban, rural), district size, and community characteristics related to district achievement.

During the development of CAT E and F. careful attention was given to ethnicity, age, and gender bias. In addition, all try–out materials were reviewed by women and men who represented various ethnic groups and who held responsible positions in the educational community. In the urban area under study, the California Achievement Test batteries were given in grades 3, 5, 6, and 8, covering the categories which will be compared: Word Analysis, Vocabulary, Comprehension, Spelling, Language Mechanics, Language Expression, Mathematics Computation, and Mathematics Concepts and Application.

DATA COLLECTION

The subjects selected for this study were at grade level 5 sometime during the last three school years and had been living in one particular urban transitional shelter. The researcher met with the School Department research assistant to discuss the collection of California Achievement Test data. It was understood by the researcher and research assistant that the information could only be given to the researcher as a blind study. The names of the subjects were given to the research assistant at the School Department. Of 20 names given to the research assistant, data for seven, over a five–month period of time, were able to be completed. Some of the subjects had never registered in the urban school system, some had never taken the CAT test battery, some were tested in one school, and a second test could not be retrieved. The seven cases were numbered from 1 through 7 and were returned to the researcher as a blind study. The name, school, and date of birth were deleted. Therefore, any of the seven cases could be any one of the 20 children whose names were submitted. The researcher applied the case study design technique and pattern–matching methods.

The question under study was: "Does a change in living environment from family unit to shelter unit have an effect on the academic performance of school–age children who have become homeless?" First, using a ten–month school calendar, a table was designed to present the results of the California Achievement Test for each case calculated in months and years.

Second, a table for the school district under study was also developed to present an evaluation summary of the fifth and sixth grade mean scores on the California Achievement Test in the categories of "Word Analysis", "Vocabulary", "Comprehension", "Spelling", "Language Mechanics", "Language Expression", "Mathematics Computation", and "Mathematics Concepts and

Application". It was necessary to know the mean score for children who were not homeless to determine what the deviation from the mean, if any, would be for the children who were homeless.

Third, a spread sheet was developed which recorded the fifth grade homeless children's data which included the district mean, the average, and the maximum and minimum California Achievement Test scores for each case. The data were then calculated to analyze how much of a deviation from the district mean score there was according to the month and year the test was administered on the fifth grade level when the school–age child was homeless. The table also recorded the average, maximum, and minimum CAT scores in each of the categories tested (Word Analysis, Vocabulary, Comprehension, Spelling, Language Mechanics, Language Expression, Mathematics Computation, and Mathematics Concepts and Application). The same information was recorded for each case when the school–age child was no longer homeless.

The data were then analyzed and calculated to determine how much of a deviation from the district mean deficit there was according to the month and year the test was administered, 5.6 and 6.6 respectively. To determine the impact of homelessness on academic performance, the calculation with a minus deviation from the district mean showed event "X" (homelessness) has an impact on "Y" (academic achievement). This links that data to the proposition that homelessness is a major problem in our urban environment and has severe consequences for the urban public school. A graph was developed depicting the total battery achievement score of each student–when they were homeless in the fifth grade and when they were returned to a family unit in the sixth grade.

Finally, the gauge for comparing the test scores while the students were homeless with the test scores after they moved into a permanent setting was done by the application of pattern–matching methodology. The fifth and sixth grade total battery scores were charted to determine if there was an effect or not. All scores were charted on or above the grade level were designated "no effect", and all scores charted below the grade level were designated "an effect". A graph was developed to demonstrate the pattern–matching methodology for the seven cases to plot academic performance in the categories of Word Analysis, Vocabulary, Comprehension, Spelling, Language Mechanics, Language Expression, Mathematics Computation, and

Mathematics Concepts and Application from the test scores. The language of the data will be discussed in the next chapter.

IV

Findings Of The Study

In view of the increasing numbers of children associated with the homelessness problem, the purpose of this study was to examine and compare yearly academic achievement scores and to identify the impact that the change in living environment from family unit to shelter unit has on the academic achievement of school–age children. It is hypothesized that homelessness adversely influences academic achievement as measured by standardized test scores.

To achieve the purpose, the study examined the California Achievement Test scores of homeless school–age children in an urban transitional shelter. Using the case study technique, the study reports and compares descriptive data of the academic achievement scores for seven school–age children during a period of homelessness and then one year later, when those same children were living in a family unit. The pattern–matching methodology was used to analyze the relationship of the academic achievement scores of the seven children who experienced homelessness with the norm scores of children who had not experienced homelessness to determine the impact of the homeless experience upon academic achievement. The specific categories examined on the California Achievement Test were: Word Analysis, Vocabulary, Comprehension, Spelling, Language Mechanics, Language Expression, Mathematics Computation, and Mathematics Concepts and Application. The categories were matched to the California Achievement Test scores when the school–age children were homeless and when they were returned to a family unit. All achievement test scores of the seven cases were matched with the school district's score on the California Achievement Test in the same categories to estimate the variance and to determine the effect of homelessness on the academic achievement of school–age children.

The results of this examination follow. First, using a ten–month school year calendar, a table was designed to present the results of the

California Achievement Test scores calculated for each case in months and years. This table for the school district under study was also developed to present an evaluation summary of the fifth and sixth grade mean scores on the California Achievement Test in the categories of Word Analysis, Vocabulary, Comprehension, Spelling, Language Mechanics, Language Expression, Mathematics Computation, and Mathematics Concepts and Application. It was necessary to know the mean score for children who were not homeless to determine what the deviation from the mean, if any, would be for the children who were homeless.

RESULTS OF EVALUATION SUMMARY

Table 1 lists the district California Achievement Test (CAT) scores for grades 5 and 6. The tests were given the sixth month of the school year. The findings for the district mean score for each category on the fifth grade level were: Word Analysis (5.1); Spelling (6.0); Reading Vocabulary (5.9); Reading Comprehension (5.7); Language Mechanics (5.6); Language Expression (5.7); Mathematics Computation (5.7); and Mathematics Concepts and Application (5.9). The district was at least five months behind in "Word Analysis" and from one month to three months ahead in the other categories of academic performance. On the sixth grade level, the district did better. The findings for the district mean scores for each category on the sixth grade level were: Word Analysis (6.5); Spelling (7.0); Reading Vocabulary (6.8); Reading Comprehension (7.5); Language Mechanics (7.8); Language Expression (7.7); Mathematics Computation (7.1); and Mathematics Concepts and Application (7.3). The district was one month behind in "Word Analysis" and from two months to fourteen months ahead in the other categories of academic performance. The entire district needs strengthening on the fifth and sixth grade levels in the category of "Word Analysis".

Table 1
School District California Achievement Test
Evaluation Summary

	WORD ANALYSIS	SPELLING	READ VOCAB	READ COMP	READ TOTAL	LANG MECH	LANG EXP	LANG TOTAL	MATH COMP	MATH C&A	MATH TOTAL
5TH GRADE EQUIVALENT	5.1	6.0	5.9	5.7	5.8	5.6	5.7	5.7	5.7	5.9	5.8
6TH GRADE EQUIVALENT	6.5	7.0	6.8	7.5	7.0	7.8	7.7	7.8	7.1	7.3	7.2

Second, a spread sheet was developed which recorded the fifth grade homeless children data. Table 2 presents the district mean and the California Achievement Test scores (average, maximum, and minimum) for the seven cases studied. The data were then calculated to analyze how much of a deviation from the district mean score there was, according to the month and year the test was administered on the fifth grade level, when the school–age child was homeless. This table also records the average, maximum, and minimum California Achievement Test scores in each of the categories tested: Word Analysis, Vocabulary, Comprehension, Spelling, Language Mechanics, Language Expression, Mathematics Computation, and Mathematics Concepts and Application.

Third, the same information was recorded for each case when the school–age child was no longer homeless and was retested in the sixth grade (see Table 3).

DATA

The data were calculated to find the average, maximum, and minimum score for each of the categories under study (Word Analysis, Vocabulary, Comprehension, Spelling, Language Mechanics, Language Expression, Mathematics Computation, and Mathematics Concepts and Application). The average scores for each category and the deviation (homeless) students are presented in Table 4.

Table 2
District Mean and "Homeless" Students' California Achievement Test Scores for Categories Tested

	District Mean	Students' CAT Scores							Avg	Max	Min
		1	2	3	4	5	6	7			
Word Analysis	5.1	2.6	1.6	1.8	6.7	1.1	4.2	4.5	3.2	6.7	1.1
Vocabulary	5.9	4.3	4.3	3.5	4.6	2.0	3.9	4.5	3.9	4.6	2.0
Comprehension	5.7	3.7	5.2	4.0	6.4	3.8	3.7	5.7	4.6	6.4	3.7
Spelling	6.0	4.2	3.6	5.1	10.2	2.9	4.0	5.8	5.1	10.2	2.9
Language Mechanics	5.6	3.4	1.5	3.7	3.3	3.1	5.3	5.3	3.7	5.3	1.5
Language Expression	5.7	2.5	2.2	6.2	8.6	2.0	2.3	4.7	4.1	8.6	2.0
Math Computation	5.7	3.4	4.3	3.9	5.6	5.7	4.5	7.4	5.0	7.4	3.4
Math Concepts & Application	5.9	3.3	3.3	4.2	4.0	3.8	3.7	7.1	4.2	7.1	3.3

Deviation from District Means

	District Mean	Students' CAT Scores							Avg	Max	Min
		1	2	3	4	5	6	7			
Word Analysis	5.1	-2.5	-3.5	-3.3	1.6	-4.0	-0.9	-0.6	-1.9	1.6	-4.0
Vocabulary	5.9	-1.6	-1.6	-2.4	-1.3	-3.9	-2.0	-1.4	-2.0	-1.3	-3.9
Comprehension	5.7	-2.0	-0.5	-1.7	0.7	-1.9	-2.0	0.0	-1.1	0.7	-2.0
Spelling	6.0	-1.8	-2.4	-0.9	4.2	-3.1	-2.0	-0.2	-0.9	4.2	-3.1
Language Mechanics	5.6	-2.2	-4.1	-1.9	-2.3	-2.5	-0.3	-0.3	-1.9	-0.3	-4.1
Language Expression	5.7	-3.2	-3.5	0.5	2.9	-3.7	-3.4	-1.0	-1.6	2.9	-3.7
Math Computation	5.7	-2.3	-1.4	-1.8	-0.1	0.0	-1.2	1.7	-0.7	1.7	-2.3
Math Concepts & Application	5.9	-2.6	-2.6	-1.7	-1.9	-2.1	-2.2	1.2	-1.7	1.2	-2.6
Average Deviation from District Mean		-2.3	-2.5	-1.7	0.5	-2.7	-1.8	-0.1	-1.5	1.3	-3.2

35

Table 3
District Mean and "Family Sheltered" Students' California Achievement Test Scores for Categories Tested

	District Mean	Students' CAT Scores							Avg	Max	Min
		1	2	3	4	5	6	7			
Word Analysis	6.5	2.8	1.2	7.1	8.4	2.8	8.1	6.2	5.2	8.4	1.2
Vocabulary	6.8	6.2	3.8	2.1	7.2	3.1	6.2	5.4	4.9	7.2	2.1
Comprehension	7.5	4.4	5.6	5.4	8.4	3.4	5.6	8.4	5.9	8.4	3.4
Spelling	7.0	5.6	5.2	7.2	9.9	5.6	5.1	9.9	6.9	9.9	5.1
Language Mechanics	7.8	3.3	2.5	3.3	5.2	5.2	10.1	5.2	5.0	10.1	2.5
Language Expression	7.7	2.5	3.0	8.7	5.5	2.3	4.8	5.1	4.6	8.7	2.3
Math Computation	7.1	5.6	6.9	5.8	7.8	6.9	5.5	7.7	6.6	7.8	5.5
Math Concepts & Application	7.3	4.6	3.3	8.0	6.5	6.1	5.6	7.8	6.0	8	3.3

Deviation from District Means

	District Mean	Students' CAT Scores							Avg	Max	Min
		1	2	3	4	5	6	7			
Word Analysis	6.5	-3.7	-5.3	0.6	1.9	-3.7	1.6	-0.3	-1.3	1.9	-5.3
Vocabulary	6.8	-0.6	-3.0	-4.7	0.4	-3.7	-0.6	-1.4	-1.9	0.4	-4.7
Comprehension	7.5	-3.1	-1.9	-2.1	0.9	-4.1	-1.9	0.9	-1.6	0.9	-4.1
Spelling	7.0	-1.4	-1.8	0.2	2.9	-1.4	-1.9	2.9	-0.1	2.9	-1.9
Language Mechanics	7.8	-4.5	-5.3	-4.5	-2.6	-2.6	2.3	-2.6	-2.8	2.3	-5.3
Language Expression	7.7	-5.2	-4.7	1.0	-2.2	-5.4	-2.9	-2.6	-3.1	1.0	-5.4
Math Computation	7.1	-1.5	-0.2	-1.3	0.7	-0.2	-1.6	0.6	-0.5	0.7	-1.6
Math Concepts & Application	0.3	-2.7	-4.0	0.7	-0.8	-1.2	-1.7	0.5	-1.3	0.7	-4.0
Average Deviation from District Mean		-2.8	-3.3	-1.3	0.1	-2.8	-0.8	-0.3	-1.6	1.4	-4.0

Table 4

Average Scores and Deviation for
Grade 5 Students When Homeless

Category	Grade 5	Deviation
Word Analysis	3.2	−1.9
Vocabulary	3.9	−2.0
Comprehension	4.6	−1.1
Spelling	5.1	−0.9
Language Mechanics	3.7	1.9
Language Expression	4.1	−1.6
Mathematics Computation	5.0	−0.7
Mathematics Concepts and Application	4.2	−1.7

The deviation ranges from a seven–month deviation in "Mathematics Computation" to a two–year deviation in "Vocabulary". The average scores for each category and the deviation for Grade 6 (returned to a family unit) students are presented in Table 5.

Table 5

Average Scores and Deviation for Grade 6 Students
When Returned to a Family Unit

Category	Grade 6	Deviation
Word Analysis	5.2	−1.3
Vocabulary	4.9	−1.9
Comprehension	5.9	−1.6
Spelling	6.9	−0.1
Language Mechanics	5.0	−2.8
Language Expression	4.6	−3.1
Mathematics Computation	6.6	−0.5
Mathematics Concepts and Application	6.0	−1.3

The average deviation ranges from −0.1 in "Spelling" to −3.1 in "Language Expression". The maximum scores for Grade 5 and Grade 6 on the California Achievement Test categories studied and the deviations are presented in Table 6. On the fifth grade level, the maximum deviation was from –1.3 to 4.2 above grade level. On the sixth grade level, the maximum scores were from 0.4 to 2.9. The minimum scores for Grade 5 and Grade 6 on the California Achievement Test categories studied and the deviations are presented in Table 7.

Table 6

Maximum Scores and Deviations for Grade 5 and Grade 6
on the California Achievement Test Categories

Category	Grade 5	Deviation	Grade 6	Deviation
Word Analysis	6.7	1.6	8.4	1.9
Vocabulary	4.6	–1.3	7.2	0.4
Comprehension	6.4	0.7	8.4	0.9
Spelling	10.2	4.2	9.9	2.9
Language Mechanics	5.2	–0.3	10.1	2.3
Language Expression	8.6	2.9	8.7	1.0
Mathematics Computation	7.4	1.7	7.8	0.7
Mathematics Concepts and Application	7.1	1.2	8.0	0.7

Table 7

Minimum Scores and Deviations for Grade 5 and Grade 6
on the California Achievement Test Categories

Category	Grade 5	Deviation	Grade 6	Deviation
Word Analysis	1.1	–4.0	1.2	–5.3
Vocabulary	2.0	–3.9	2.1	–4.7
Comprehension	3.7	–2.0	3.4	–4.1
Spelling	2.9	–3.1	5.1	–1.9
Language Mechanics	1.5	–4.1	2.5	–5.3
Language Expression	2.0	–3.7	2.3	–5.4
Mathematics Computation	3.4	–2.3	5.5	–1.6
Mathematics Concepts and Application	3.3	–2.6	3.3	–4.0

The minimum scores on each category gives the maximum deviation from 1.6 on "Mathematics Computation" to 5.3 on "Word Analysis".

Fourth, interpretation of findings for each case was done by the application of pattern–matching methodology. The fifth and sixth grade total pattern scores were charted to determine if there was "an effect" or not. All scores charted at or above the grade level were designated "no effect", and all scores charted below the grade level were designated "an effect". A graph was developed to demonstrate the pattern–matching methodology for the seven cases to plot academic performance in the categories of Word Analysis, Vocabulary, Comprehension, Spelling, Language Mechanics, Language Expression, Mathematics Computation, and Mathematics Concepts and Application from the test scores. Following will present an analysis of the results in each of these categories.

"WORD ANALYSIS" CATEGORY

The items in the "Word Analysis" category measure understanding of structural word parts and word forms. The student identifies initial or final cluster and digraph sounds, vowel sounds, and diphthongs or variant vowel sounds. Also measured are recognition of sight words, inflectional endings, and compound words.

In grade 5, the result of homelessness on academic performance in the category of "Word Analysis" was severe. Only Subject #4 scored above district average; the others scored from one year to four years behind. The scores indicate that a change in living environment from a family unit to a shelter unit has "an effect" on the academic performance of school–age children who have become homeless from approximately six months to four years. In grade 6, three subjects scored above the district grade equivalent and one subject scored a point below the level. Subjects #4 and #6 have made at least a two–year advancement. (See Figure 1.)

"VOCABULARY" CATEGORY

The items in the "Vocabulary" category measure same–meaning, opposite–meaning words, and words in context.

The severity of the impact of homelessness on academic performance in the category of "vocabulary" was from one to three years below the grade level. Subject #4 scored just above the district grade equivalency; Subjects #2 and #3 had scores lower than their fifth grade scores. Scores increased for Subjects #1, #6, and #7, but were still lower than the district grade equivalency. In the category of

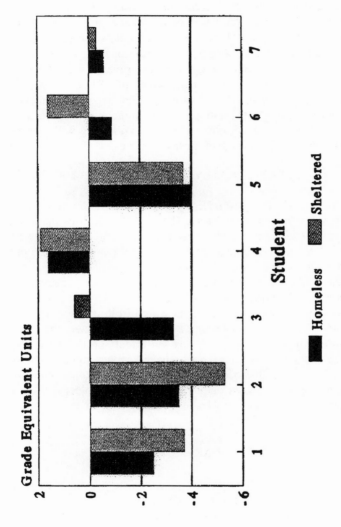

Figure 1. Students' "Word Analysis" Scores -- Deviation from District Mean.

"Vocabulary", the change in living environment from family unit to shelter unit had "an effect" on the academic performance of school–age children who became homeless. (See Figure 2.)

"COMPREHENSION" CATEGORY

The items in the "Comprehension" category measure comprehension of reading passages. Items test the student's ability to extract details, analyze characters, identify main ideas, and interpret events described in passages.

The severity of the impact of homelessness on academic performance in the category of "Comprehension" was from six months to two years below grade level for four of the subjects. One subject was one grade level, and Subject #4 was above grade level. On the sixth grade level, five students were from one to three years below grade level, and two were above the district grade equivalency. In the category of "Comprehension", a change in living environment from family unit to shelter unit had "an effect" on the academic performance of school–age children who became homeless. (See Figure 3.)

"SPELLING" CATEGORY

The items in the "Spelling" category measure application of spelling rules for consonants, vowels, and various structural forms. Items are presented in the context of sentences with a missing word. The student identifies the correct spelling of the word to complete the sentence.

The severity of the impact of homelessness on academic performance in the category of "Spelling" was from six months to two years below grade level. On the sixth grade level, three students tested from six months to three years above grade level. (See Figure 4.)

"LANGUAGE MECHANICS" CATEGORY

The items in the "Language Mechanics" category measure skills in the mechanics of capitalization and punctuation.

The severity of the impact of homelessness on academic performance in the category of "Language Mechanics" was from two to five years below grade level. In the category of "Language Mechanics" on the fifth grade level, there was "an effect" for five out

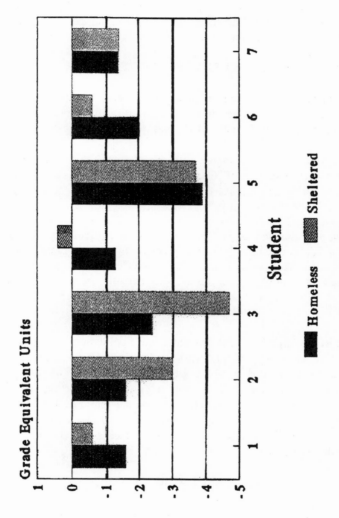

Figure 2. Students' "Vocabulary" Scores -- Deviation from District Mean.

42

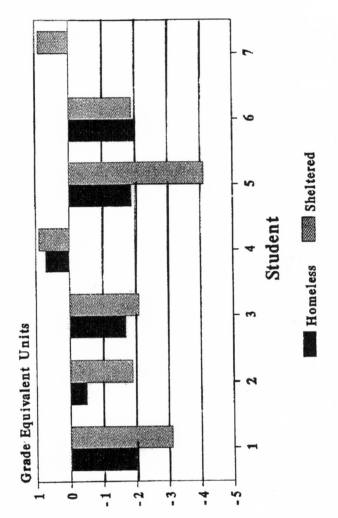

Figure 3. Students' "Comprehension" Scores -- Deviation from District Mean.

43

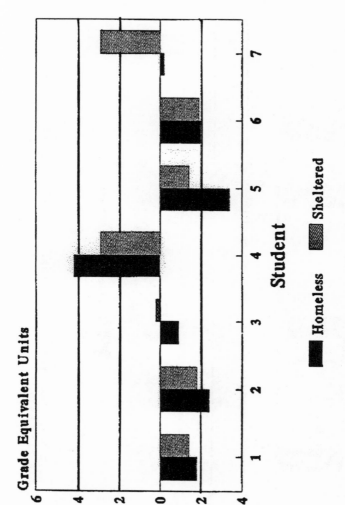

Figure 4. Students' "Spelling" Scores -- Deviation from District Mean.

of seven students on academic performance from one month to four years from the district mean due to the change in living environment from family unit to shelter unit. On the sixth grade level, six out of seven students were affected from two to five years from the district mean. (See Figure 5.)

"LANGUAGE EXPRESSION" CATEGORY

The items in the "Language Expression" category measure skills in language usage and sentence structure. Items require identification of the correct noun, pronoun, verb, or adjective that completes a sentence. Other items require identification of correct sentence structure, including substituting the correct pronoun for nouns in a sentence and changing a statement to a question. All items in the test are based on rules of written standard English.

"Language Expression" appeared to be the category of academic performance most severely impacted by homelessness. While homeless, four out of seven subjects were at least three years below grade level. One subject was one year below the district equivalency level. On the sixth grade level, all subjects were from two years to five years below the grade level and the district grade equivalency. The change in environment from family unit to shelter unit had "an effect" on the academic achievement of school–age children who were homeless and then returned to a sheltered unit. (See Figure 6.)

"MATHEMATICS COMPUTATION" CATEGORY

The items in the "Mathematics Computation" category measure computation skills in addition and subtraction of whole numbers.

"Mathematics Computation" appeared to be the category of academic performance least severely impacted by homelessness. One subject was two years below grade level; three subjects were a few months to one year below grade level; and three subjects were above grade level or close to the district grade equivalency on both the fifth and sixth grade levels. (See Figure 7.)

"MATHEMATICS CONCEPTS AND APPLICATION" CATEGORY

The items in the "Mathematics Concepts and Application" category measure understanding of mathematics concepts. Specific skills

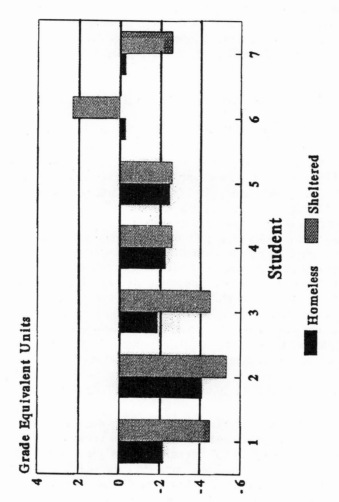

Figure 5. Students' "Language Mechanics" Scores -- Deviation from District Mean.

46

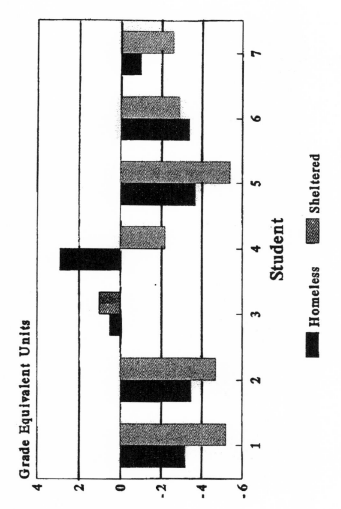

Figure 6. Students' "Language Expression" Scores -- Deviation from District Mean.

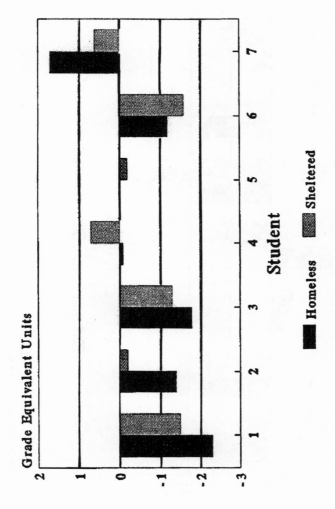

Figure 7. Students' "Mathematics Computation" Scores --
Deviation from District Mean.

48

include concepts dealing with numeration, problem solving, measurement, and geometry.

"Mathematics Concepts and Application" was a category severely impacted by homelessness on the average of two years below grade level. On the fifth grade level, students were one to three years below the district grade equivalent. The change in living environment from family unit to shelter unit had "a definite effect" on the academic performance of school–age children who became homeless. (See Figure 8.)

CASE CALIFORNIA ACHIEVEMENT TEST SCORES: HOMELESS VS. FAMILY SHELTERED

The data were analyzed and calculated to determine how much of a deviation from the district mean deficit there was according to the month and year the test was administered, 5.6 and 6.6 respectively. To determine the impact of homelessness on academic performance, the calculation with a minus deviation from the district mean showed event "X" (homelessness) had an impact on "Y" (academic achievement). This links the data to the proposition that homelessness was a major problem in our urban environment and had severe consequences for the urban public school.

For case–by–case results of the academic achievement scores for seven school–age children during a period of homelessness and a year later, when these same children were living in a family unit, the pattern–matching methodology was used to analyze the relationship of the academic achievement scores of the seven children who had a homeless experience to determine the impact of the homeless experience upon academic achievement.

In grade 5, the scores in the following categories are: Word Analysis (2.6), Vocabulary (4.3), Comprehension (3.7), Spelling (4.2), Language Mechanics (3.4), Language Expression (2.5), Mathematics Computation (3.4), and Mathematics Concepts and Application (3.3).

CASE 1

The deviation from the district mean scores in each category are: Word Analysis (–2.5), Vocabulary (–1.6), Comprehension (–2.0), Spelling (–1.8), Language Mechanics (–2.2), Language Expression (–

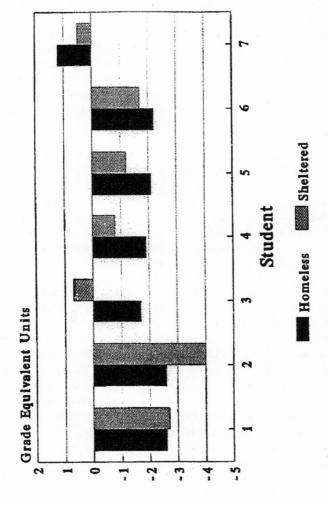

Figure 8. Students' "Mathematics Concepts and Application"
Scores -- Deviation from District Mean.

50

3.2), Mathematics Computation (–2.3), and Mathematics Concepts and Application (–2.6).

In grade 6, the scores in the following categories are: Word Analysis (2.8), Vocabulary (6.2), Comprehension (4.4), Spelling (5.6), Language Mechanics (3.3), Language Expression (2.5), Mathematics Computation (5.6), and Mathematics Concepts and Application (4.6). The deviation from the district mean scores in each category are: Word Analysis (–3.7), Vocabulary (–3.1), Comprehension (–1.4), Spelling (–4.5), Language Mechanics (–5.2), Language Expression (–5.2), Mathematics Computation (–1.5), and Mathematics Concepts and Application (–2.7).

The student was below the district mean 1½ years in "Vocabulary" skills to three years behind in "Language Expression". Even when this student returned to a family unit, he or she could only do better in the categories that he or she could focus on for short periods of time and be successful. This student's deviation from the district mean demonstrates that special services were needed while he or she was living in a homeless shelter. (See Figure 9.)

CASE 2

In grade 5, the scores in the following categories are: Word Analysis (1.6), Vocabulary (4.3), Comprehension (5.2), Spelling (3.6), Language Mechanics (1.5), Language Expression (2.2), Mathematics Computation (4.3), and Mathematics Concepts and Application (3.3). The deviation from the district mean scores in each category are: Word Analysis (–3.5), Vocabulary (–1.6), Comprehension (–0.5), Spelling (–12.4), Language Mechanics (–14.1), Language Expression (–3.5), Mathematics Computation (–1.4), and Mathematics Concepts and Application (–2.6).

In grade 6, the scores in the following categories are: Word Analysis (1.2), Vocabulary (3.8), Comprehension (5.6), Spelling (5.2), Language Mechanics (2.5), Language Expression (3.0), Mathematics Computation (6.9), and Mathematics Concepts and Application (3.3). The deviation from the district mean scores in each category are: Word Analysis (–5.3), Vocabulary (–3.0), Comprehension (–1.9), Spelling (–1.8), Language Mechanics (–5.3), Language Expression (–4.7), Mathematics Computation (–0.2), and Mathematics Concepts and Application (–4.0).

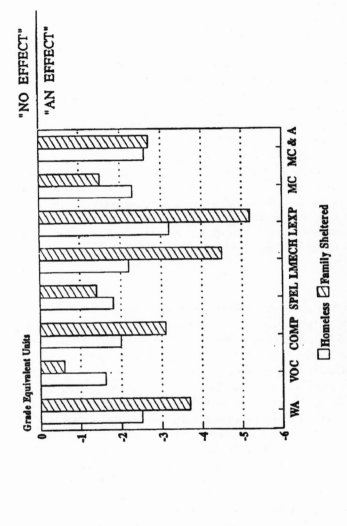

Figure 9. Student 1 California Achievement Test Scores (Homeless vs. Family Sheltered).

52

The student was below the district mean from two months to four years. This student was minimally behind in his or her ability to analyze reading comprehension and mathematics computation. Therefore, this student should have been able to do well academically. This student appeared to have been traumatized by being homeless. After the student returned to a family unit, he or she became from one year to one and one–half years more deviant from the district mean.

Only in the category of "Spelling" did this student show marked improvement, again documenting that traumatized students have the feeling of being lost and can only focus on subjects that last for short time periods and bring a fast measure of success. Progress was also made in "Mathematics Computation" which shows they could answer questions on lessons presented that day. (See Figure 10.)

CASE 3

In grade 5, the scores in the following categories are: Word Analysis (1.8), Vocabulary (3.5), Comprehension (4.0), Spelling (5.1), Language Mechanics (3.7), Language Expression (8.7), Mathematics Computation (5.6), and Mathematics Concepts and Application (8.0). The deviation from the district mean scores in each category are: Word Analysis (–3.3), Vocabulary (–2.4), Comprehension (–1.7), Spelling (–0.9), Language Mechanics (–1.9), Language Expression (0.5), Mathematics Computation (–1.8), and Mathematics Concepts and Application (–1.7).

In grade 6, the scores in the following categories are: Word Analysis (7.1), Vocabulary (2.1), Comprehension (5.4), Spelling (7.2), Language Mechanics (3.3), Language Expression (8.7), Mathematics Computation (5.8), and Mathematics Concepts and Application (5.6). The deviation from the district mean scores in each category are: Word Analysis (0.6), Vocabulary (–4.7), Comprehension (–2.1), Spelling (0.2), Language Mechanics (–4.5), Language Expression (1.0), Mathematics Computation (1.3), and Mathematics Concepts and Application (0.7).

The student was below the district mean by two years in every category except "Vocabulary". The year this student returned to a family unit, this student scored above the district mean in the categories of "Word Analysis", "Spelling", and "Language Expression". (See Figure 11.)

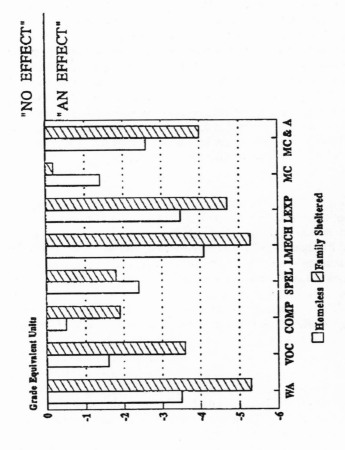

Figure 10. Student 2 California Achievement
Test Scores (Homeless vs. Family Sheltered).

CASE 4

In grade 5, the scores in the following categories are: Word Analysis (6.7), Vocabulary (8.4), Comprehension (9.9), Spelling (5.2), Language Mechanics (5.2), Language Expression (8.6), Mathematics Computation (5.6), and Mathematics Concepts and Application (4.0). The deviation from the district mean scores in each category are: Word Analysis (1.6), Vocabulary (–1.3), Comprehension (0.7), Spelling (4.2), Language Mechanics (–2.3), Language Expression (2.9), Mathematics Computation (0.1), and Mathematics Concepts and Application (–1.9).

In grade 6, the scores in the following categories are: Word Analysis (8.4), Vocabulary (7.2), Comprehension (8.4), Spelling (9.9), Language Mechanics (5.2), Language Expression (2.3), Mathematics Computation (6.9), and Mathematics Concepts and Application (6.1). The deviation from the district mean scores in each category are: Word Analysis (1.9), Vocabulary (0.4), Comprehension (0.9), Spelling (2.9), Language Mechanics (–2.6), Language Expression (–2.2), Mathematics Computation (–0.7), and Mathematics Concepts and Application (–0.8).

The student was below the district mean in all categories while he or she was homeless except for the areas that if a student were not absent from school the student could conceivably do well in, such as "Vocabulary", "Language Mechanics", and "Mathematics Concepts and Application". (See Figure 12.)

CASE 5

In grade 5, the scores in the following categories are: Word Analysis (1.1), Vocabulary (2.0), Comprehension (3.4), Spelling (2.9), Language Mechanics (3.1), Language Expression (2.0), Mathematics Computation (5.7), and Mathematics Concepts and Application (3.8). The deviation from the district mean scores in each category are: Word Analysis (–4.0), Vocabulary (–3.9), Comprehension (–'.9), Spelling (–3.1), Language–Mechanics (–2.5), Language Expression (–3.7), Mathematics Computation (0.0), and Mathematics Concepts and Application (–2.1).

In grade 6, the scores in the following categories are: Word Analysis (2.8), Vocabulary (3.1), Comprehension (5.6), Spelling (5.2), Language Mechanics (5.2), Language Expression (2.3), Mathematics

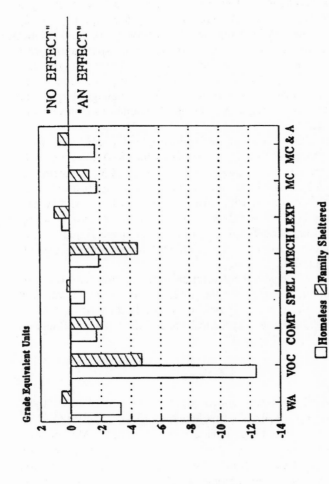

Figure 11. Student 3 California Achievement
Test Scores (Homeless vs. Family Sheltered).

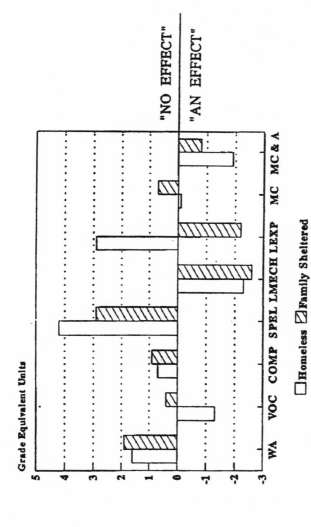

Figure 12. Student 4 California Achievement Test
Scores (Homeless vs. Family Sheltered).

57

Computation (6.9), and Mathematics Concepts and Application (–2.1). The deviation from the district mean scores in each category are: Word Analysis (–3.75), Vocabulary (–3.7), Comprehension (–4.1), Spelling (–1.4), Language Mechanics (–2.6), Language Expression (–5.4), Mathematics Computation (–0.2), and Mathematics Concepts and Application (–1.2).

The student was below the district mean from two years to four years in every category while homeless, except for the category of "Mathematics Computation". When this student returned to a family unit, the score only improved in "Spelling" and "Mathematics Concepts and Application", two areas where the student could have immediate success if he or she were able to focus for short periods of time. (See Figure 13.)

CASE 6

In grade 5, the scores in the following categories are: Word Analysis (4.2), Vocabulary (3.9), Comprehension (3.7), Spelling (4.0), Language Mechanics (5.3), Language Expression (2.3), Mathematics Computation (4.5), and Mathematics Concepts and Application (–3.7). The deviation from the district mean scores in each category are: Word Analysis (–0.9), Vocabulary (–2.0), Comprehension (–2.0), Spelling (–0.3), Language Mechanics (–0.3), Language Expression (–3.4), Mathematics Computation (–1.2), and Mathematics Concepts and Application (–2.2).

In grade 6, the scores in the following categories are: Word Analysis (6.1), Vocabulary (6.2), Comprehension (5.6), Spelling (5.1), Language Mechanics (10.1), Language Expression (2.3), Mathematics Computation (5.5), and Mathematics Concepts and Application (5.6). The deviation from the district mean scores in each category are: Word Analysis (–1.6), Vocabulary (–0.6), Comprehension (–1.9), Spelling (–1.9), Language Mechanics (2.3), Language Expression (–2.9), Mathematics Computation (–1.6), and Mathematics Concepts and Application (–1.7).

The student was below the district mean from six months in "Language Mechanics" to three and one–half years in "Language Expression" in all categories, while living in the transitional shelter. When this student returned to a family unit, he or she scored above the district mean in the categories of "Word Analysis" and "Language Mechanics". It would appear from these test results that this student

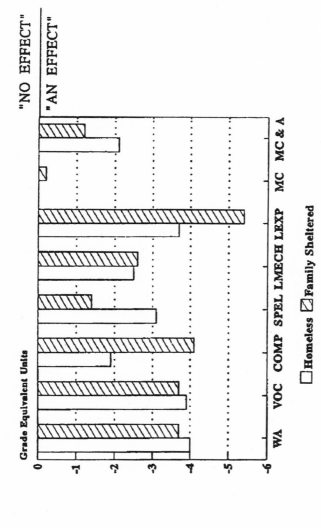

Figure 13. Student 5 California Achievement Test Scores (Homeless vs. Family Sheltered).

59

understood how to structure word parts and form words and there should be some carry–over in the other categories. However, this student remained with a deviation of minus six months to three years in the other categories. (See Figure 14.)

CASE 7

In grade 5, the scores in the following categories are: Word Analysis (4.5), Vocabulary (4.5), Comprehension (5.7), Spelling (5.8), Language Mechanics (5.3), Language Expression (4.7), Mathematics Computation (7.4), and Mathematics Concepts and Application (7.1). The deviation from the district mean scores in each category are: Word Analysis (–0.6), Vocabulary (–1.4), Comprehension (–0.0), Spelling (–0.2), Language Mechanics (–0.3), Language Expression (–1.0), Mathematics Computation (–1.7), and Mathematics Concepts and Application (1.2).

In grade 6, the scores in the following categories are: Word Analysis (6.2), Vocabulary (5.4), Comprehension (8.4), Spelling (9.9), Language Mechanics (10.1), Language Expression (5.2), Mathematics Computation (5.1), and Mathematics Concepts and Application (7.8). The deviation from the district mean scores in each category are: Word Analysis (–0.3), Vocabulary (–1.4), Comprehension (0.9), Spelling (2.9), Language Mechanics (–2.6), Language Expression (–2.6), Mathematics Computation (0.6), and Mathematics Concepts and Application (0.5).

This student was from one month to two and one–half years below the district mean in the categories of "Word Analysis", "Vocabulary", "Language Mechanics", and "Language Expression" when the student was homeless. This student's strengths are in the categories of "Reading Comprehension" and "Mathematics Computation". Therefore, it appears that this student was severely impacted by being homeless because when he or she returned to a family unit, the scores in both "Mathematics Computation" and "Mathematics Concepts and Application" were lower. He or she only improved greatly in the category of "Spelling", which is the category that one can focus on for the shortest period of time and have immediate success on the weekly spelling test. (See Figure 15.)

The findings of the individual cases showed diminution of academic achievement when both improvement and diminution ere observed in one or more categories for every case as hypothesized.

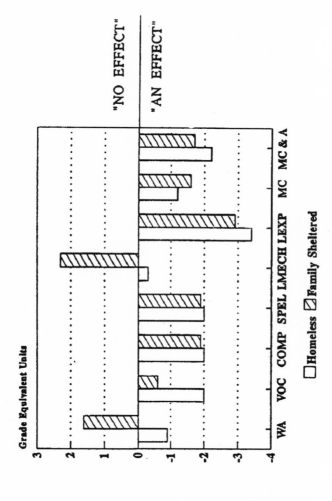

Figure 14. Student 6 California Achievement Test Scores (Homeless vs. Family Sheltered).

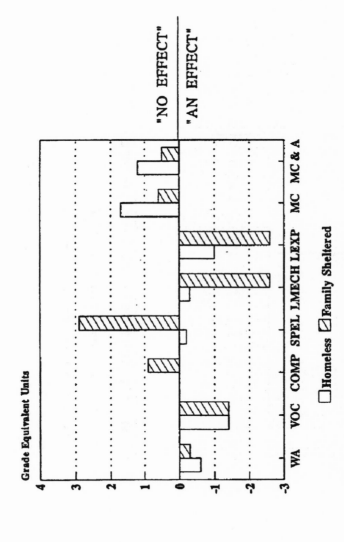

Figure 15. Student 7 California Achievement Test Scores (Homeless vs. Family Sheltered).

Therefore, the finding of this proposition is that homelessness is a major problem in our urban environment as noted in each case under study.

SUMMARY OF THE FINDINGS

Research suggests that homeless children may experience difficulty with language, sustained attention to task, physical coordination, as well as developmental delays.

The findings of this study agree with the suggestion that homeless children experience difficulty with language. The students under study tested from one and one–half years deviation to two years deviation from the district mean in the categories of "Word Analysis", "Vocabulary", "Language Mechanics", and "Language Expression". On the total battery, the homeless tested from seven months to two years on the mean scores. When the children returned to a family–sheltered unit without the intervention of special educational services, the overall battery results remained approximately the same. In other words, the effect of being homeless extended over a period of six months to a year, as shown by a greater deviation from the district mean. The findings also agree with the research suggestion that school–age students, who have been homeless because of the rootlessness of homelessness, need manageable work assignments scheduled for short periods of time that they could handle with success. The category of "Spelling" resulted in the lowest deviation on the district mean after being returned to a family unit.

This study focused on changes in academic achievement scores of homeless school–age elementary children as reflected by their annual California Achievement Test scores. The study suggests agreement with the hypothesis that school–age children who are homeless need special educational services to address their specific needs while they are homeless.

V

Discussion, Summary, Conclusion And Recommendations

The first section of this chapter restates the problem. The second section presents a summary of the procedures and a summary of the findings. The conclusions reached are discussed in the third section. The fourth section focuses on recommendations for practice and future research.

DISCUSSION

One of our nation's most critical problems today is homelessness. Over the past decade, the nature of this problem has changed by the growth of divergent subgroup populations which now include many families. Sixty percent of the homeless are families with children, and most of these children are of elementary school age. Annual estimates of the number of homeless school–age children in the United States range from 310,000 to 1.6 million. The U. S. Department of Education estimated that in 1989, 273,000 school–age children were homeless at some time during the year and that 28 percent of these children did not attend school during the time they were homeless. The failure of a child to attend school is one of many direct consequences of the parents' homelessness (New Jersey Department of Education, 1991).

Poverty seems to have a strong influence on homelessness. The apparent effects of poverty appear to relate to the lack of a sufficient education, both of which are effects of the circumstances and characteristics of homelessness. Homeless school–age students represent a population of our children who are most at risk. The younger children are at risk (according to Alperstein and Arnstein, 1988; Miller and Lin, 1988; Bassuk, 1985; and Bassuk and Rubin,

1987), for three basic reasons:
1. Inadequate health care, along with the lack of immunization;
2. Increased levels of anxiety and depression;
3. Delay in general development, specifically language development.

The school–age homeless children needs are complex, and they face many challenges because of their homelessness. They seem to have a pattern of moving from shelter to shelter, consequently interrupting their schooling and opportunities for social development. Breakey and Fisher (1990) state that many school–age children belong to single–parent families; and even when both parents are with the family, the father may be banished at night because the shelter where they are staying cannot accommodate men. The hypothesis involved is: Homelessness adversely influences academic achievement as measured by standardized test scores.

SUMMARY OF THE PROCEDURE

The California Achievement Test (CAT) was used to access the academic achievement of school–age children who were homeless living in a transitional setting. The instrument used for testing was the California Achievement Test, Forms E and F. published by McGraw Hill in 1985. This series of tests was designed to measure achievement in the basic skills commonly found in state and district curricula. They provide information about the relative ranking of students against a norm group, as well as specific information about the instructional needs of students.

The subjects selected were at grade level 5 sometimes during the last three school years, and had been living in one particular urban transitional shelter. The researcher met with the School Department research assistant to discuss the collection of California Achievement Test data. It was understood by the researcher and research assistant that the information could only be given to the researcher as a blind study. The names of the subjects were given to the research assistant at the School Department. Out of 20 names given to the research assistant, data for seven were able to be completed.

Some of the subjects had never registered in the urban school system, some had never taken the CAT test battery, some were tested in one school, and a second test could not be retrieved. Because of the issue of confidentiality, cases were numbered from 1 through 7 and were returned to the researcher as a blind study. The name, school, and date of birth were deleted. Therefore, any of the seven cases could be one of the 20 children whose names were submitted. The researcher applied the case study design technique and pattern–matching methodology to analyze and calculate how much of a deviation from the district mean there was according to the month and year the test was annually administered. To determine the impact of homelessness on academic performance, the calculation with a minus deviation from the district mean showed event "X" (homelessness) has an impact on "Y" (academic achievement). This links that data to the proposition that homelessness is a major problem in our urban environment and has severe consequences for the urban public school.

SUMMARY OF THE FINDINGS

The subjects continued to experience an academic lag in their achievement. That is to say, even though they returned to a stabilized setting, the deficiency continued to be evidenced by a six–month to one–year deviation from the district mean. Sabastian (1985), Bassuk (1985), and Eddowes and Hranity (1989) suggest that homeless children may experience difficulty with language, sustained attention to task, physical coordination, as well as developmental delays.

The findings of this study agree with the suggestions that school–age children who have been homeless experience difficulty with language. The students under study (tested between a one–year to a five–year span) showed "an effect" deviation from the district mean scores in the categories of "Word Analysis", "Vocabulary", "Language Mechanics", and "Language Expression."

The findings of this study also agree with the findings of Rafferty and Rollins (1989), and Molnar, Rate, and Klein (1990) that children who have been homeless suffer psychological and emotional damage due to circumstances that usually accompany homelessness. These children need manageable work assignments scheduled for short periods of time that they can manage with success. The categories of "Spelling" and "Mathematics Computation" showed the smallest "an effect" deviation from the district mean score of the categories tested. These two can be presented in small, manageable work assignments. The findings of this study agree that school–age children who are homeless experience developmental delays. Even when the school–age children returned to a family–sheltered unit, in six categories under study the "an effect" deviation from the mean increased instead of decreased.

The conceptual pattern for the study was that homelessness has an impact on the academic achievement of school–age children. The academic achievement scores of the homeless child fall below the norm of those of children without the experience of homelessness. The operational pattern for this study (i.e., the independent variable) was the scores of the academic achievement observed in each of the categories of the California Achievement Test and related to the norm for that grade. A match between these patterns for the study was the analysis of the independent and dependent variables.

In this study, the data were calculated in years and months to analyze how much of a deviation there was from the district mean scores on the standardized California Achievement Test in the categories tested: Word Analysis, Vocabulary, Comprehension, Spelling, Language Mechanics, Language Expression, Mathematics Computation, and Mathematics Concepts and Application.

CONCLUSION

Although findings of this study are restricted to a particular district at one time period, they are certainly suggestive. They suggest the need for continued research in the area. In addition, when combined with the findings of Rafferty and Rollins (1989) and Maza and Hall (1988), the researcher would argue that they present a compelling case for supportive education in order for homeless school–age children to at least maintain normal academic achievement levels.

Any child not achieving at the mean average for the district score was in need of assistance, and any negative deviation would be considered significant. (For example, from the study, a child who was 1.9 months behind in "Mathematics Concepts and Application" was in need of assistance as was a child who was 2.6 years behind.) If the child was above the mean average, the achievement score was insignificant. A child who was one month behind might just need quiet time to do his or her work. Another child who showed a year or two behind may need an individual remediation program designed to address his or her specific needs. Even though the homeless school–age child may have the same deviation as the so–called normal school–age child, the deviation from the mean was more significant for homeless school–age children because they have less support in other areas of their lives. The psychological implications of homelessness (i.e., low self–esteem, rootlessness, stress, and trauma) are barriers to academic achievement. The socioeconomic implications of homelessness (i.e., residence in dangerous environments, difficulties in meeting the basic needs of food, adequate clothing, and safety) are barriers to academic achievement. The educational implications of homelessness (i.e., absenteeism, placement in inappropriate programs, lack of transportation and adequate records) are barriers to academic achievement. The political implications of homelessness (i.e., where the student attends school, comparable educational service, transportation, and parent participation) all mitigate against an atmosphere of successful academic achievement.

Unfortunately, but obviously, many homeless children are in a state of crisis. They may have lived with their families on the streets for months in condemned or otherwise inadequate buildings and in chaotic and violent situations. Whitman, Accardo, Boyert, and Kendagar (1990) suggest that the homeless child's capacity to sit and attend, to process and recall, and to answer test questions in a classroom situation may be further impaired by the emotional and transitional nature of their crisis situation. Frequent moves result in multiple school transfers, with learning time lost with each transfer. Often children are not enrolled in school while the family lives in a temporary shelter. Such temporary stays can last several months, and the cumulative effect of lost school time contributes to further academic underachievement, grade retention, and gaps in learning and experience. Even when homeless children go to school, they may find it difficult to find space and time for homework in a shelter, thereby being set up for failure due to circumstances beyond their control–a precursor to learned helplessness.

For these children, the school environment could serve as a stable, cognitive and emotional support that is unavailable elsewhere. Instead, too often the school becomes a part of the problem. Behavior difficulties, learning problems, and emotional reactivity are attributed to homelessness with the result that underlying treatable retention problems and learning disabilities remain undiagnosed. Stereotyping and labeling by teachers and peers is a common phenomenon. Often, the children become further isolated as a result of a cycle–of labeling, reactivity, and more labeling. Even when children have obvious problems and are referred for testing, they may move before the testing is completed or the results available. Each move brings a new school, a new referral, and further delays. Ultimately, the children may never be effectively identified as needing special educational services. Thus, the very children who need special educational services to maximize their potential are doubly penalized by the inappropriateness of their school's resource teachers, social workers, and test administrators. Homelessness is detrimental to a person's body, mind, and spirit.

Not having a home affects a person's self–image, sense of family, and sense of community. Homelessness has political, socioeconomic, psychological, and educational implications and has become a nationwide issue which threatens the foundation of American society. Ultimately, this nation must provide decent, affordable housing for everyone. Until this national goal can be achieved, our major task as educators will be to rescue these families, particularly the children, from a life of deprivation and violence, and thus interfere with this newly–emergent cycle of intergenerational homelessness.

RECOMMENDATIONS FOR PRACTICE AND FUTURE RESEARCH

Based on the findings of this study, the following recommendations are made for the use of transitional shelters, social service agencies, school districts, and state and federal educational agencies:

RECOMMENDATION 1

To ensure that homeless children and youth have access to free and appropriate public education, each local education agency (LEA) should take responsibility for ensuring that all homeless school–age children and youth attend school by:

1. Designating staff who are responsible for ensuring that all homeless school–age children and youth are enrolled in school and are receiving appropriate educational services; and
2. Establishing systems of communication between social service providers and school districts which ensure that homeless school–age children are enrolled in and attending school.

RECOMMENDATION 2

To ensure that all homeless students receive educational services comparable to services offered to other students, including educational programs such as compensatory, bilingual, and special education programs:

• Develop timely identification and assessment procedures of homeless student educational needs in order to provide required services. Technical assistance should also be provided by the school system to service providers to ensure that homeless students receive appropriate educational services; and
• Develop and adopt policies and practices to ensure that homeless children and youth are not isolated and stigmatized.

RECOMMENDATION 3

Revise any federal, state, or local laws, regulations, policies, or practices that may act as barriers to enrollment, attendance, or success in school for homeless school–age children and youth:

Review and revise laws and regulations to comply with the Stewart B. McKinney Homeless Assistance Amendments Act of 1990 (P.L. 101–645). In order to achieve this goal, the focus should be on reviewing the following procedures:

• Parent consultation
• Choice of educational placement
• Record transfer and enrollment procedures
• Timeliness for enrollment
• Identification of homeless students
• Use of educational service emergency referral form
• Transportation policies

RECOMMENDATION 4

To assist local education agencies (LEAs) and providers in developing and implementing transportation and school district transfer systems which meet the needs of homeless students:

1. Explore funding sources and coordinate services to help LEAs and providers provide transportation to homeless school–age children and youth;
2. Establish specific strategies addressing school and health records and timeliness that would result in timely registration and immediate entrance of homeless students to school;
3. Encourage LEAs and providers to assist homeless families in maintaining school and health records and obtaining proper immunization.

RECOMMENDATION 5

To assist in the development and coordination of programs which will provide supplementary supportive services, including health, nutrition, recreation, and social services for homeless students:

The school should facilitate the establishment of networks with nutritional health, recreational, and counseling agencies. The federal and state educational departments should develop and administer grants to school districts and service providers for the development of programs which address the educational, physical, social, and psychological needs of homeless children and youth, which may include the following:

- Tutoring
- Counseling services
- Enrichment activities
- Recreational activities
- Summer programs, nutritional support, health and hygiene counseling, and sports involvement

RECOMMENDATION 6

To coordinate the establishment of linkages between social service agencies, school districts, advocacy groups, and other state agencies in order to effectively meet the needs of school–age homeless children and youth:

1. Disseminate to school districts resource lists of social services providers;
2. Participate in committees and conferences which deal with homeless school–age children and youth issues;

3. Participate in national and regional meetings to develop systems of information exchange and problem resolution.

RECOMMENDATION 7

Develop and implement training programs for school districts and services:

1. Examine linkages between county welfare agencies and school districts which facilitate identification and enrollment of homeless school–age children and youth;
2. Investigate and implement systems whereby homeless students of the working poor and doubled–up families are identified and receive appropriate educational services;
3. Identify and develop a statewide list of social service providers and services that address the comprehensive needs of homeless and runaway youth;
4. Assess the needs of school districts and service provider personnel;
5. Coordinate training programs with service providers to elicit their perspectives and enlist their participation;
6. Conduct training programs for school personnel to heighten awareness of and sensitivity to the specific educational needs of homeless school–age children and youth.

RECOMMENDATION 8

Programs should be developed to increase public awareness of and sensitivity to the issues surrounding homelessness and its effects on school–age children and youth:

1. Develop programs which will create awareness of the effects of homelessness on children and youth;
2. Identify key community groups and agencies through which to present awareness programs;
3. Workshops should be conducted in collaboration with other agencies, service providers, parents, and community groups on the educational issues surrounding homelessness;
4. Develop opportunities for homeless or previously homeless parents to address groups about their experiences of homelessness;
5. Support and encourage public awareness initiatives on the needs of homeless children and youth.

VI

Further Discussion On Homelessness And Selected Innovative Programs

The foregoing study has shown the impact of homelessness on the academic achievement among young people. It also suggests the dramatic impact homelessness has on the lives of children and their parents. As an educator and one committed to dealing with social and educational ills of homelessness, it would be unfair to leave this at the level of statistics and case studies.

In fact, there have been studies of these matters and suggestions for reform and certain kinds of innovative programs. The researcher will, therefore, conclude this study by discussing the issues of homelessness as presented by the Office of Education in Pennsylvania and by outlining a few of (what she considers) the most significant innovative programs. Discussion in this chapter is not intended as definitive but simply as suggestions of alternatives to the recommendations based upon the data of this study.

FURTHER DISCUSSION ON HOMELESSNESS

The Pennsylvania Office of Education defines four educational issues of homelessness and some supportive strategies which could be considered and utilized by educators:

1. The issue of constantly moving has the following effects on homeless school–age children: Rootlessness; no sense of their space or possessions; sees life as temporary; leaves projects half finished; clings to possessions; restless; aggressive behavior as they try to claim something for themselves; feels loss of control in other areas of their lives so they will literally fight for control at school; frustration; difficulty with transitions; poor attention span. The intervention strategies:

- Give the children something that belongs only to them (e.g., a plant, ball, or game); others must ask their permission to play or work with this possession.
- Break tasks down into small segments that can be successfully completed in a short period of time; keep a checklist of completed work; contract with students to finish projects and assignments. The experience of mastery and achievement is critical to their self–esteem.
- Teach them to act responsibly in the classroom and expect responsible behavior from them (e.g., you are responsible for books, keeping cubbies clean).
- Teach them alternative ways to express frustration (e.g., talk to someone or into a tape recorder, take a voluntary "time out" and remove yourself from the situation to work on an art project).
- Include defined transition procedures as you move from one activity to the next. ("We have 10 minutes left in this math period.") Provide closure for the children if you know in advance they are leaving the school. Give them time to clean out their cubby or locker and say "Good–Bye" to friends and school staff. Give them a copy of their transfer card and IEP (if they have one) when they leave.

2. The issue of frequent change of schools has the following effects on homeless school–age children: No structure in their lives; lack of continuity; unwillingness to risk forming deep partnerships; use of withdrawal and introversion as a defense; depression over leaving familiar places and friends; may fall behind academically as they miss school days and change curricula and teachers; may be placed inappropriately because of lack of school records. The intervention strategies:

   - Provide structure in the classroom by keeping a consistent daily schedule and clear, concise rules posted so that they are visible at all times. Let the children know if you are planning to have a substitute the following day.
   - Assign children a "buddy" to help them learn their way around the school. Involve them in cooperative learning activities.
   - To quickly integrate the children into the appropriate classroom, have a set of quickly–administered assessment

tools available for use in placing the children if their records have not arrived.

- Ensure that the children have access to all educational services for which they might be eligible, including Chapter I and bilingual programs.

3. The issue of overcrowded one–room living situations (lack of private space and limited space for physical activities) has the following effects on homeless school–age children: Withdrawal or aggressive behavior; unable to do homework because of noisy environment, adults, and lack of physical space; behind academically; unable to get enough sleep; constantly tired and listless; learn to tune others out; hyperactivity and delays in gross motor development. The intervention strategies:

- Be aware that these children may listen and attend to important information with some difficulty. Use various modalities for presenting important information (i.e., say it, write it on the chalkboard, have children repeat it).
- Provide a portable lap desk (sturdy box to take their work home in and to use as a writing surface).
- Do not use the children's recess or Physical Education times as a make–up or detention period; they may not have space in the motel or shelter to run, jump, and play.

4. The issue of lack of access to basic resources has the following effects on homeless school–age children: Insufficient clothing; reluctance to attend school because they view their clothes as substandard; may be stigmatized by peers; low self–esteem; lack of refrigeration/cooking facilities; parents have to purchase food daily, which is expensive–means less food can be purchased, putting children at nutritional risk; gastroenteritis (due to ingestion of harmful bacteria from unclean eating utensils); uncontrollable diarrhea; anemia; general weakened condition making child more vulnerable to upper respiratory infections, asthma, and ear infections which may lead to delayed language development; lack of transportation; inability to keep medical appointments; lack of medical and pre–natal care; may take two to three buses to get to school; parents living outside district boundaries may be stretching to the limit to get children; may arrive late, missing school breakfast program. The intervention strategies:

- Keep the child's living situation confidential; bolster self–esteem by providing an opportunity to pursue non–academic activities at which he or she can succeed; determine strengths and build on these; keep clean, pressed clothes available to give to the children (in a subtle manner) as needed.
- Make sure the children and their parents are aware of free lunch and breakfast programs offered by your school; help them sign up, without publicly asking for a show of hands of those needing free lunch; keep a few nutritious snacks available for those children who miss breakfast.
- Do not penalize the children for being late; arrange the first period so that they will not miss key learning material if they arrive late; ensure that they càn participate in field trips and school–wide activities if they do not have transportation or necessary fees.
- If you celebrate birthdays in your classroom with treats, look for alternative ways to provide goodies for this child's party for those parents who may not be able to afford or may not have the facilities to make those treats.

SELECTED INNOVATIVE PROGRAMS

This section presents profiles of several innovative programs which are providing educational and supportive services to homeless families with school–age children. The programs profiled are sponsored by states, school districts, and community–based organizations. Each program is working up to address school access and placement issues as well as working with other service providers to develop more comprehensive services. Zeldin and Bogart (1990), with this framework, describe innovative ways in which services are being offered to homeless students and their families.

STATE OF MARYLAND

Helping Hands Homework Assistance Program

The State of Maryland's Office of Education for Homeless Children and Youth, in cooperation with the State of Maryland's Office for

Library Services, is working to match libraries throughout the State with shelters to conduct after–school educational support for homeless children to study, read, and work on school projects. Participating children also receive daily homework assistance for one to two hours from high school students who are paid for their services. The activities at each library are supervised by a paid teacher who serves as an adult mentor.

Statewide School Days Drive

The Statewide School Days Drive was initiated in Maryland to (1) address the problems resulting from inadequate school supplies available to homeless children; (2) establish partnerships between schools and shelters; and (3) sensitize school officials and local communities about the needs of homeless students. Phase I, known as the "Governor's Care Enough to Share Project", was held for a week in early August. At that time, all state employees were encouraged to collect school supplies for homeless students. Phase II, "Students Helping Students", was held in October. This project matched community shelters with local schools whose students were encouraged to donate children's books, coloring books, crayons, dictionaries, novels, and educational games to participating shelters.

Operation Partnership

Operation Partnership encourages cooperation among family shelters and elementary schools in Maryland. The State Homeless Coordinator provides awareness sessions for shelter and school staff. Each session focuses on the conditions in each local jurisdiction and includes dialogues among service providers and visits to a local shelter. In addition, slides of pictures drawn by homeless children are reviewed to identify issues pertaining to self–esteem and competency among homeless youth. *Population Served*: In 1988–1989, the State of Maryland reported 3,795 homeless school–age children and youth.

STATE OF TEXAS

Programs are being developed and administered by the Office of Assistance to Homeless Children. Immunization records showed the low enrollment of homeless children in school. In response to this concern, the Texas Education Agency (TEA) developed a system to assist homeless children in enrolling in school, by immunizing them and maintaining their school records. The TEA then established a statewide data base with immunization records of each homeless student, which districts can use by calling a toll–free number. Individual numbers are assigned to protect the confidentiality of each child. Eventually, education as well as health–related service information is included in the statewide data base. *Population Served*: In 1989–1990, the State of Texas reported an estimated 20,000 homeless school–age children.

Local Education Agencies (LEAs): District efforts of the Allentown School District (ASD) Services were coordinated by the Director of Pupil Personnel Services. To address enrollment delays, ASD first worked to increase awareness of district staff about the needs of homeless children and explain the legal requirements for providing services. Workshops were held for administrators, secretaries, teachers, and shelter providers. Procedures were established to allow students to remain in their home schools during periods of homelessness. When children do change schools, new procedures ensure the quick transfer of immunization and student records between school districts. For example, initial confirmation of student records can be made over the telephone, and schools and shelters are using a standard form for release of information. School is viewed as the one thing that can be stable for children during a period of homelessness.

STATE OF WISCONSIN

Madison (Wisconsin) Metropolitan School District

The Madison (Wisconsin) Metropolitan School District operates transitional services for homeless children to facilitate re–entry into public school. When Madison first began to have a homeless population, one elementary school served all of the district's homeless children. The school became proficient in serving homeless students, sufficient assessment, providing emotional support to students, and effectively mainstreaming students into the school. When the number of students grew, it became necessary for the school system to establish a transition room for homeless children staffed by a teacher, a psychologist, and an aide.

Although a child's stay in the transition room is brief, it provides an opportunity to become adjusted to the school (materials, supplies, etc.) and to meet the principal and teachers. A psychologist conducts assessments and provides counseling to address each student's emotional needs and fears. Concurrently, the teacher and teacher assistant test the children to determine grade level and grade placement, help parents fill out registration forms, and inform and prepare the classroom teacher who will be instructing the child. Transition room staff are also responsible for service coordination and follow–up when a student leaves the school. The staff meet with their counterparts in the child's new school to pass along assessment information and academic records, and to describe the source of materials and intercultural approaches used in the transitional classroom.

STATE OF NEW JERSEY

Newark (New Jersey) School District

The Burent Street Elementary School of the Newark (New Jersey) School District is identified in response to an increase in the number of homeless families and in recognition of the difficulties inherent in administering an educational program for a transient homeless population in Newark. The Board of Education of Newark, New Jersey, has chosen to concentrate its resources primarily on one school, which the Board has determined does not have adequate resources or expertise. Burent Street Elementary School was selected to serve as a magnet school because of its proximity to a number of homeless shelters, hotels, and the homeless population it was already serving. Throughout the City, homeless children are now bused to Burent Street Elementary School. Additional staff hired include three attendance counselors (who report daily to shelters and homeless hotels), a social worker, a psychologist, a learning disabilities specialist, and a part–time nurse. A planning committee, headed by an assistant superintendent, meets monthly to plan and manage resources for the school.

The businesses in Newark have established partnerships with the School and provide transportation funding for field trips. The partnership sponsor operates an after school tutorial program for homeless children in the second grade. A key club at a suburban school recently "adopted" Burent Street Magnet School. Members have donated clothing and have hosted a party for the children. *Population Served*: The majority of the students are residents of four hotels that house homeless families.

STATE OF CALIFORNIA

The Harbor Summit School

The Harbor Summit School is a self–contained, shelter–based elementary school administered by the San Diego (California) County Office of Education. The school has three classrooms serving students in grades K–1, 2–4, and 5–8. Each class is staffed by a full–time teacher and teaching assistant. Additionally, a paraprofessional aide provides tutoring services most of each week. Students attend school four and one–half hours each morning. A legal teacher/aide ratio of 8–to–1, supplemented by computer–assisted instruction, allows students to progress at their own pace. In the afternoon, students from the shelter participate in after–school activities, including arts and crafts, outdoor recreation, and field trips within the community. *Population Served*: The program serves all resident children who are eligible for grades 1–8.

The Grace Hill Family Center (Non–Profit Organization Model)

The Grace Hill Family Center provides shelter–based educational services for parents and children within the context of a large community action program. The Grace Hill Family Center is a more supportive program that provides transitional housing and support services to children. It also assists parents in supporting their children educationally. Other services are aimed at assisting children in their transition to school. *Population Served*: The Grace Hill Family Center has a capacity of 42 persons, of which 65 percent are children and adolescents. Over 1,000 persons are served annually.

The above sample of innovative programs which are providing services to meet the needs of homeless families and school–age children implement the Stewart B. McKinney Act (P.L. 100–77). Each program addresses a critical need in that particular educational environment, and each has been successful in addressing the needs of homeless school–age children and youth.

All of these programs are certainly in accordance with the recommendations of the present study and should provide the basis for educators to attack one of the central social issues in America today–homelessness and its impact upon our children.

Appendix

1. Bandeira, Denise R. Evaluation of a Training Program for Street Children and Adolescents At Risk in Brazil. *Paper presented at the Annual InterAmerican Congress of Psychology, San Juan, Puerto Rico*, 1995.

2. Bullard, Sara. Where the Heart Is. A Seattle Principal Redefines Schooling, Re–Creates Home for Children in Poverty. *Teaching Tolerance,* 1993.

3. California. The State of our Children. *Data Supplement Children Now*, Oakland, CA, 1993.

4. Center for Law and Education. Materials on the Education of Homeless Children, *Harvard University*, 1991.

5. Daniels, Judy. Humanistics Interventions for Homeless Students; Identifying and Reducing Barriers to Their Personal Development. *Journal of Humanistic–Education and Development*, 1995.

6. Dohrn, Bernadine. A Long Way Home: Chicago's Homeless Children and the Schools: A report prepared from *The Homeless Advocate Project*, Exhibits B, F, G and I., 1991.

7. Education–Evaluation–and–Policy–Analysis. A summary of the educational rights of homeless children and youth afforded by the Stewart B. McKinney Homeless Assistance Act., 1995.

8. Education and Urban Society, 1993.

9. Helm, Virginia M. Legal Rights to Education of Homeless Children and Youth, 1993.

10. Horner, Mary P. (1992). Nevada's Children: Selected Educational and Social Statistics. *Nevada State Dept. of Education*, 1992.

11. Horowitz, Sandra. The Coping Strategies of Homeless Children and Adolescents. *Paper presented at the Biennial Meeting of the Society for Research in Child Development*, 1991.

12. Michigan State Board of Education. A Manual for Implementation of the Stewart B. McKinney Homeless

13. Assistance Amendments Act; *Lansing Office* for the Education of Homeless Children and Homeless Youth, 1991.

14. North Carolina State Dept. of Public Instruction, Raleigh. A Closer Look. Report of the Task Force on the Achievement of Culturally Diverse Students, 1992.

15. Policy Studies Associates, Inc. (1992). Serving Homeless Children: The Responsibilities of Educations. *Washington, D.C.*, 1992.

16. Rafferty, Yvonne. And Miles To Go....Barriers to Academic Achievement and Innovative Strategies for the Delivery of Educational Services to Homeless Children. *Advocate for Children of New York Inc. Long Island City.*, 1991.

17. Root, Elaine H. Educational Responses to Issues of Self–Esteem and Trust in Homeless Students. *Masters Research Paper*, University of North Texas, 1990.

18. Rubin, David H. and Others. Cognitive and Academic Functioning of Homeless Children Compared with Housed Children. *Pediatrics*, 1996.

19. Schwartz, Wendy. School Programs and Practices for Homeless Students. *Eric/CUE Digest*, No. 105, 1995.

20. Wiley, David C; Ballard, Danny J. How Can Schools Help Children from Homeless Families? *Journal of School Health*, 1993.

Bibliography

Alperstein, G., & Arnstein, E. (1988). Homeless children: A challenge for pediatricians. *The Pediatric Clinics of North America*, 35, 1413–1425.

Baster, B. (1985, December 12). Homeless families staying in offices. *The New York Times*.

Bassuk, E. L. (1985). *The feminization of hopelessness: Families in Boston shelters*. Paper presented at the annual meeting of the American Association of Social Psychiatry, Boston, MA.

Bassuk, E. L., & Rubin, L. (1987). Homeless children: A neglected population. *American Journal of Orthopsychiatry*, 57, 279–286.

Bowen, J. M. et al. (1989, March 27). *Educating homeless* children and Youth: A Policy analysis symposium. Paper presented at the annual meeting of the American Educational Research Association.

Breakey, W. R., & Fisher, P. J. (1990, Winter). Homelessness: The extent of the problem. Journal of Social Issues, (4), 31–48.

California Achievement Test, Forms E and F (CAT E and F). (1985). New York: McGraw–Hill Book Company.

Campbell, D. J. (1975, July). Degrees of freedom and the case study. *Comparative Political Studies*, 8, 178–193.

Campbell, D. J., & Fiske, D. W. (1959). Convergent and discriminant validation by the multitrait–multimethod matrix. *Psychological Bulletin*, 56, 81–105.

Campbell, D. J., & Stanley, J. C. (1963). Experimental and quasi–experimental design for research on teaching. In N. L. Gage (Ed.), *Handbook of research on teaching*. Chicago, IL: Rand McNally.

Coalition for the Homeless. (1984). *Perchance to sleep:* Homeless children without shelter in New York City. New York: Coalition for the Homeless.

Coles, R. (1976). *Uprooted children*. Pittsburgh, PA: University Press

Cook, J. D., & Campbell, D. J. (1979). *Quasi–experimental: Design and analysis issues for field settings.* Chicago, IL: Rand McNally.

Cronbach, L. J. et al. (1980). *Toward reform of program evaluation aims method and institutional arrangements.* San Francisco, CA: Jossey Bass.

Cronbach, L. J., & Meehl, P. E. (1955). Construct validity in psychological tests. *Psychological Bulletin*, 52, 281–301.

Eddowes, E. A., & Hranity, J. R. (1989, October). Educating children of the homeless. *The Education Digest.*

Frawley, R., & Zafonte, S. M. (1984, October). *Meeting the needs of homeless Youth: A report of the Homeless Youth Steering Committee.* New York: New York State Council on Children and Families.

Geivertzman, R., & Fodor, I. (1987, May–June). The homeless child at school: From welfare hotel to classroom. Child Welfare Leaques of America, 66(3).

Cuba, E. G., & Lincoln, Y. S. (1981). *Effective evaluation.* San Francisco, CA: Jossey–Bass.

Herbert, M. (1985). *Children of the welfare hotels.* New York: Citizens Committee for Children of New York.

Human Resource Administration of New York City. (1985). *Longitudinal study of homeless families.* New York: Human Resource Administration of New York City.

Jacobs, G. (1970). *The participant observer: Encounter with social reality.* New York: Braziller.

Kilman, G. (1986). *Psychological emergencies of childhood.* New York: Griene and Stratton.

Kozol, J. (1988, January 25). Rachel and her children: The homeless and their children. *New Yorker*, 65–84.

Krim, A. (1982). *Families after fire: Trauma over time.* Paper presented at the annual meeting of the American Medical Association, New York.

Levin, I. (1984, July). Homelessness: Its implications for mental health. Policy and Practice, 8(1).

Maza, P. F., & Hall, J. A. (1988). *Homeless children and their families: A preliminary study.* Washington, D. C.: Child Welfare League of America.

McKinney, S. B. (1985). CTB/McGraw Hill. Monterey, CA: McGraw Hill, Inc.

McKinney, S. B. (1987, July 22). Stewart B. McKinney Homeless Assistance Act (P.L. 100–77).

McKinney, S. B. (1988, November 7). Stewart B. McKinney Homeless Assistance Amendments Act of 1988 (P.L. 100–629).

McKinney, S. B. (199Q). Stewart B. McKinney Homeless Assistance Amendments Act of 1990 (P.L. 101–645).

Miller, D S., & Lin, H. B. (1988). Children in sheltered homeless families: Reported health status and use of health services. *Pediatrics*, 81, 668–673.

Molnar, J. M., Roth, R., & Klein, T. P. (1990, Winter). Constantly compromised: The impact of homelessness on children. *Journal of Social Issues, 46*(4), 109–124.

Mowbray, C. J. (1985, January). Homelessness in America: Myths and realities. *American Orthopsychiatrist, 55*(1).

New Jersey Department of Education. (1991). *A plan for state action.* New Jersey: New Jersey Department of Education.

Patton, M. Q. (1980). *Qualitative evaluation methods.* Beverly Hills, CA: Sage.

Rafferty, Y., & Rollins, N. (1989). *Learning in limbo: The educational deprivation of homeless children.* New York: Advocates for Children of New York.

Redburn, F., & Terry, B. F. (1986). *Responding to American homeless public policy alternatives.* New York: Praeger Publishers.

Scientific America. (1984, July).

Sebastian, J. G. (1985, November). Homelessness: A stage of vulnerability. *Family and Community Health.*

Trochim, W. M. K. (1985, October). Pattern matching, validity, and conceptualization. *Evaluation Review*, 9(5), 575–604.

U. S. Department of Education. (1989). Report to Congress on state interim reports on the education of homeless children. Washington, D. C.: U. S. Department of Education.

U. S. General Accounting Office. (1990, April 24). Charles A. Bowsler, Comptroller General of the United States. Washington, D. C.: U. S. General Accounting OffiCe

Washinqton Post Maqazine. (1988, May 29).

Wells, A. S. (1990, April). Educating homeless children. *Eric Clearinghouse on Urban Education Digest*, 30–32.

Whitman, B. Y., Accardo, P., Boyert, M., & Kendagar, R. (1990, November). Homelessness and cognitive performance in children: A possible link. *Social* Work, 35(6), 516–519.

Wilson, M. (1989, April). Mommie, when can we go home? *World Vision.*

Yin, R. K. (1984). *Case study research design and methods.* Beverly Hills, CA: Sage Publications, Inc.

Zeldin, S., & Bogart, J. (1990, January). *Education community support for homeless children and youth: Profiles of fifteen innovative and promising approaches.* New York: Policy Studies Association, Inc.

Index

DATE DUE
